Bilhana

Bilhana

Wholefood Recipes From Egypt, Lebanon, And Morocco

Yasmine Elgharably
Shewekar Elgharably

Photographs by
Yehia El-Alaily

The American University in Cairo Press
Cairo New York

**Special thanks
go to Sarah Ibrahim,
Ahmed Ammar, Amr Agami.**

First published in 2021 by
The American University in Cairo Press
113 Sharia Kasr el Aini, Cairo, Egypt
One Rockefeller Plaza, 10th Floor, New York, NY 10020
www.aucpress.com

Text © 2021 by Yasmine Elgharably and Shewekar Elgharably

Photographs © 2021 by Yehia El-Alaily

Dar el Kutub No. 13354/18
ISBN 978 977 416 907 6

Dar el Kutub Cataloging-in-Publication Data

Elgharably, Yasmine
    Bilhana: Wholefood Recipes from Egypt, Lebanon, and Morocco / Yasmine
Elgharably, Shewekar elgharably.—Cairo: The American University in Cairo Press, 2021.
    p.   cm.
    ISBN 978 977 416 600 6
    1.   Cooking, Middle Eastern
    641.5956

1 2 3 4 5   24 23 22 21

Designed by Sherif ElKomy and Tarek Yehia
Printed in China

Contents الفهرس

The Authors 6
About the Book 7
In Your Pantry 8
Breakfast & Mezze 15
Soups & Stews 57
Salads, Pulses, & Grains 75
Veggies & Greens 109
Roasts & Grills 135
From the Sea 169
Sweet Things 187
Drinks 211
Index 229

The Authors

Shewekar Elgharably is a certified Holistic Health Coach and a Culinary Nutrition Expert based in Cairo, Egypt. She completed the Integrative Nutrition Program and the Culinary Nutritional Expert Program at the US-based Academy of Culinary Nutrition. Originally an established interior designer, after seeing how small food and lifestyle changes have a huge impact on health, she wanted to help people strive to live healthier and happier lives. Shewekar is also the founder of #HealthyRocks.

Yasmine Elgharably is a self-taught home cook with a business background and a huge passion for Middle Eastern food. She is the founder of and a partner in CairoCooking.com, a recipe sharing platform aiming to help home cooks share recipes and cooking ideas across the Middle East. She is also based in Cairo, Egypt.

The Photographer

Yehia El-Alaily is an Egyptian–British commercial photographer based in Cairo, Egypt. His portfolio covers a wide range of trends: food, interiors, people, nature, and architecture. Meanwhile, his commercial and editorial work has been published by The Food Print 2012, 2013, and 2014, Starwood Hotels and Resorts, The Four Seasons Hotels, Hilton Worldwide, Sanctuary Retreats, Hyperallergic art magazine, Abercrombie & Kent, Nestlé, and Henkel.

About the Book

'Bilhana!' is an Arabic expression meaning 'Bon Appetit!', one that rings out in every Egyptian home. It sums up the Egyptian love of food and gathering to eat, of sharing meals with family and friends. Whether it be an extravagant dinner party, an informal brunch, or a simple weeknight meal, food is at the very center of social interaction.

We were born and raised in Cairo, Egypt, where we both still live, and come from a family of home cooks. The recipes in this book are inspired by our love of cooking, our passion for sharing food and recipes, and our rich culinary heritage. Based around the traditional dishes we grew up eating, we have added a modern, fresh take—swapping in quinoa for rice or baking rather than frying our falafel—and incorporated flavors and styles taken from other Middle Eastern cuisines, from Lebanon to Morocco.

While nutrition and healthy eating are priorities for us, dishes that do not compromise on taste and that can be part of our everyday cooking are cornerstones of our food philosophy, as reflected in the recipes in this book.

In Your Pantry

When cooking, please always try to invest in the best-quality ingredients and the freshest produce. Also, try to keep your cooking organic and chemical-free. All our recipes are based on organic, clean and pesticide-free measures; an organic egg is smaller than a regular egg, for example. And remember that fruits and vegetables are at their most nutritious, as well as freshest, when eaten in their proper season; they'll make your cooking more flavorful and your dishes more affordable.

There's barely a savory recipe in this book (not to mention some of the sweet ones) that does not use olive oil, sea salt, and freshly ground black pepper. These are essential pantry ingredients. "Extra-virgin" olive oil seems to have taken supermarket shelves by storm, but don't be taken in by the hype: a versatile, good-quality all-purpose olive oil is so much better for you than a cheap extra-virgin. And when we say "salt and pepper," we always mean, for preference, sea salt (less processed than table-grade) and freshly ground black peppercorns. If you've never paid much attention to the freshness and quality of your peppercorns, we urge you to do so; it will be a revelation. We also always prefer filtered water over bottled (or tap) water, as we find it tastes fresher and purer, plus, avoiding plastic bottles will, of course, reduce waste.

In our part of the world, of course, spices rule: ground coriander and cumin, cinnamon, cardamom, bay leaves, sumac, and chili powder keep their flavors well in the pantry, especially when you buy the best quality. Other flavor-building ingredients that we always have to hand for salad dressings and rubs are mustard, tahini (sesame seed paste), pomegranate molasses, and apple cider vinegar or white vinegar. The latter tends to be the vinegar of choice in our region, because it is not derived from alcohol, but in other parts of the world you must be sure to buy distilled white vinegar, the grade suitable for consumption. Natural sweeteners that are recommended and keep well on the shelves are raw honey, molasses, date syrup, and vanilla extract, along with fiber-full and energy-boosting raisins and dried dates.

Grains, legumes, and pulses are staples in any healthy pantry and easily stored. Brown lentils and freekeh are our favorites, as you will see in our recipes. Quinoa, red and white, and brown rice are good standbys, too, when you need a fast and filling side or salad. We also like to keep one or two sorts of nuts such as walnuts, pine nuts, or almonds to toast and sprinkle on salads or caramelize for desserts.

As for fresh ingredients, herbs, especially parsley, cilantro, mint, and thyme are mainstays of healthy Middle Eastern cooking, and arugula will give you the base for a salad any time. In our mild climate, we're so lucky to have fresh, locally grown herbs, salads, and greens almost all year-round. We grow them in our gardens or raise them in pots, and in the markets and stores they're sold loose or in bunches; there's no place for tired,

poor-quality veg to hide. If you can avoid buying bagged supermarket leaves and herbs, then do so, not least because of concerns about plastics and food-miles. Fresh leaves, washed and drained, and folded in a clean dish towel or kitchen paper, will keep in the fridge for up to five days. Other fresh ingredients on our regular shopping list are lemons and limes; pomegranates (such a great source of iron and antioxidants); onions, white and red; green onions or scallions, and—always—plump, firm bulbs of garlic. All these are must-haves to create the dishes in our book, or indeed any Middle Eastern recipe.

This book largely abstains from dairy; one exception is ghee (clarified butter), because all the lactose-containing milk solids have been removed. Like coconut oil, it's a heathy choice for frying; it doesn't denature at high temperatures to produce free radicals, as some vegetable oils do. But for creaminess and richness, we rely on oat and nut milks and butters. We occasionally use goat's feta, which has a lower lactose content than cow's milk and can be less likely to provoke allergies.

And, remember, *the freezer is your friend*!

For raw ingredients . . .

Fresh whole ginger, peeled garlic cloves, and sliced fresh chili peppers hold up pretty well in the freezer; just grate or sprinkle them straight into the pan. You can also keep sliced bread and flatbreads; they take minutes to defrost in the oven or toaster. Bone broth and stocks lend themselves to being prepared in large batches, so are perfect for your freezer. They will defrost in as little as 2–3 hours in the fridge, and once defrosted will keep, refrigerated, for up to 3 days.

And for your finished dishes . . .

Make large batches, portion them up, and let them cool thoroughly before putting them in the freezer. Make sure they're well packed (especially meat dishes) to avoid smells and leaks onto other foods. Invest in some good-quality stainless steel or glass freezer containers, better for the environment (by reducing plastic waste) but also prevent leaching from plastics into your food. When you freeze liquids, leave a gap at the top to allow for them expanding as they freeze. Label your stored items with names and cooking dates so you know which are best consumed first, and don't refreeze food after it has been defrosted. If you're using frozen meat for any of the recipes here, make sure that it is thoroughly defrosted before you start to cook.

Equipment that just makes it all easier . . .

The smoothie craze has resulted in a new breed of power blender that can handle most raw veggies as well as soft fruit, and unlike a traditional juicer, helps preserve all that valuable fiber. A hand-held or stick blender is also a lifesaver, instantly creaming your sauces and soups. Our favorite gadget, however, has to be our food processor. A really good-quality, robust model is so well worth the investment, chopping and combining your ingredients with ease, whether whipping up a big batch of hummus or creating delicious nut butters. A mini-food processor is also a great little tool that will encourage you to eat healthy and fresh even on the busiest days. Use it to chop fresh herbs and nuts to add vibrancy and extra nutrients to your salad bowl, or conjure up a zesty salsa for grilled meats; when a handful of tomatoes can be puréed in seconds, why reach for a bottle or can? Our final choices would be a really good, sharp grater to make light work of zesting limes and mincing fresh ginger and garlic, and a grinder, to get your fresh coffee and nuts to just the consistency you like.

All the food shot for this book was eaten;
none was wasted or thrown away.

Breakfast
& Mezze

Easy Lentils with Parsley

عدس بجبة بالبقدونس

 vegan protein-packed

Lentils are such an underused food considering their high nutritional values; they're full of natural protein and fiber. Lentils are easy to prepare and lend themselves to so many delicious recipes, from soups to salads. Simply cooked, they make a nourishing bowl of goodness for a warming breakfast or lunch on the go. This is our basic recipe for perfectly cooked, tasty brown lentils. It can be served warm or cold, and will keep in an airtight container in the fridge for up to 3 days.

You can add variety by adding all sorts of toppings: arugula, red onions, colored peppers, beets, and most herbs all partner lentils well. For a more substantial dish, add in some cooked chickpeas for the last 5 minutes of cooking.

Makes: 4 servings

250 g (8 oz) brown lentils
1 onion, quartered
2 tomatoes, 1 quartered and 1 diced
1 teaspoon ground cumin
Salt and pepper
60 ml (¼ cup) olive oil
Juice of 2 limes
Small bunch parsley, stems removed and finely chopped (about ½ cup)

Time: 45 minutes

Wash the lentils in a sieve under cold running water. Place them in a large pan and cover with fresh water. Add the onion, quartered tomato, cumin, and salt and pepper to taste. Bring to the boil, then lower the heat to a simmer and cover. The lentils should cook in about 20–25 minutes; make sure not to overcook them into a mush.

Drain any excess liquid from the lentils, dispose of onion and tomato quarters, and place in a large bowl. Drizzle over the olive oil and lime juice, and adjust the seasoning if necessary. Just before serving, stir in the diced tomato and fresh parsley.

Hummus Three Ways

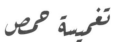

 vegan   protein-packed   🌾 gluten-free

There can hardly be a mezze menu in the Middle East that doesn't feature comforting, nourishing hummus. We make it all the time, so we like to add variety: plain, green and fragrant with fresh herbs, or red (actually a pretty pink) with warming peppers. For a large gathering, a batch of each would give your table a festive look. You can use 2 400 g cans of chickpeas, but you must rinse them well under cold running water to remove all the preservative residues.

Makes: mezze for 6

500 g (1 lb 2 oz) dry chickpeas
4 garlic cloves
4 tablespoons tahini paste
Flesh of one baked sweet potato
    (about ½ cup)
Juice of 4 limes
2 teaspoons ground cumin
½ teaspoon paprika
1 tablespoon salt
1 teaspoon pepper
125 ml (½ cup) olive oil
Sumac, to garnish (optional)

For green hummus:
Large bunch of cilantro, stems
    removed
Large bunch of parsley, stems
    removed
Handful of dill
1 teaspoon ground coriander
2 tablespoons olive oil
For red hummus:
2 red bell peppers
1 tablespoon olive oil
Another ½ teaspoon paprika
Salt and pepper

Time: 1 hour + overnight soaking time

Rinse the dry chickpeas thoroughly, cover with lukewarm water and soak overnight.

When you're ready to cook, drain the chickpeas and put them in a large pot. Cover with fresh water and bring to the boil. Lower the heat, cover the pot, and simmer for about 40 minutes, or until the chickpeas are cooked through.

While the chickpeas cook, preheat the oven to 180°C (350°F/Gas mark 4) and place the garlic cloves on an oven tray and roast in the oven for 10 minutes. Peel and leave to cool.

Drain the chickpeas, reserving about 125 ml (½ cup) of the cooking liquid. Set aside about ½ cup of the chickpeas, and put the rest in a food processor. Add the roast garlic, tahini, sweet potato, lime juice, cumin, paprika, and salt and pepper to taste.

Pulse the food processor, occasionally using a spatula to free any chickpeas stuck at the sides and base. Add the olive oil, and pulse until smooth. If the hummus is still too thick, add a little of the chickpea cooking liquid (or fresh water, if using canned chickpeas) while pulsing.

Hummus Three Ways (cont.)

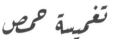

To serve, scatter over the reserved cooked chickpeas, a drizzle of olive oil, and, if you like it, a generous sprinkle of sumac.

To make green hummus:
Finely chop the green herbs and, while pulsing the chickpeas in the food processor, add them in together with the coriander and olive oil.

To make red hummus:
Preheat the oven to 180°C (350°F/Gas mark 4). While the chickpeas are cooking, halve and deseed the peppers, place them skin-side-up on an oven tray, brush with olive oil, and roast in the oven for about 25 minutes. Leave them to cool before removing the skin (it will fall off easily now) and roughly slice. Toss with the paprika, salt, and pepper. Once the chickpeas are in the food processor, add the peppers and pulse until the hummus turns pink.

Spiced Beans with Tahini

فول متبل بالطحينة

 vegan 　　 protein-packed

No other dish is as truly Egyptian as spiced fava beans. The nation's street food, breakfast, lunch, and dinner is super-filling and nutritious, rich in vegan protein. It is generally flavored with oil and lime juice, cumin, coriander, salt, and pepper, sometimes with added tomatoes, onions and parsley, or powdered chilis or fresh peppers. In all cases, you only add spices and other ingredients once the beans are cooked through. The cooking process is lengthy, so we always make a large batch; any leftover will keep in the fridge for up to a week. You can also use 1 400g can of fava beans, drained and rinsed to remove the preservatives.

Makes: 6 servings

250 g (8 oz) dried fava (broad) beans
1 onion, cut into large chunks
100 g (3 ½ oz) yellow lentils
1 tablespoon salt
½ tablespoon pepper
115 g (4 oz) tahini paste (about ½ cup)
Juice of 4 limes
1 ½ teaspoon ground cumin
1 teaspoon ground coriander
60 ml (¼ cup) olive oil, or more to taste
Small bunch of parsley, stalks removed and finely chopped (about ½ cup)
Cooked chickpeas, to garnish

Time: 4 hours + overnight soaking time

Wash the dried beans under cold running water, place in a large pan or bowl, cover with cold water and leave to soak overnight.

To cook, drain the beans then place them in a large, heavy-bottomed pan and cover with cold water. Bring to the boil, then lower the heat and let simmer for a few minutes. You will find that this first batch of water is developing a white frothy layer. Drain the beans over the sink, rinse them again, and put them back in the pan and cover with fresh water.

Bring to the boil again, then cover, lower the heat, and simmer for 3 ½ hours, until the beans are almost ready. Every 30 minutes or so, check and add boiling water as necessary to keep the beans covered.

After 3 ½ hours, add the yellow lentils and the salt and pepper. Bring back to a simmer and cook, covered, for a further 30 minutes, while you prepare the tahini mix.

In a medium bowl, mix the tahini with 4 tablespoons hot water, lime juice, cumin, and coriander, and a little salt and pepper. Whisk until smooth (add a little more hot water if necessary).

When the beans are done, put them in a food processor and pulse to break them up a little, but don't blend them smooth—the dish needs some texture. Tip into a large serving bowl, and drizzle the olive oil over the top. Add the tahini sauce and half of the parsley and fold them in to combine. Finish by scattering over the rest of chopped parsley and the chickpeas, and serve warm.

Bessara

بصارة

📎 vegan   🍶 protein-packed   🌾 gluten-free

This is a traditional Egyptian dish full of fiber, vegan protein, and nutrients from the beans and herbs. Economical and filling, it's a classic standby for the end of the month when the family budget is squeezed. But you'll find it served anytime in Egyptian homes, simply because it's so delicious, whether scooped up with warm flatbread or a crusty loaf, or served with a salad or sliced vegetables.

Bessara will keep for up to a week in the fridge, or a month in the freezer.

Makes: 8 servings

500 g (1 lb 2 oz) dried split fava
   (broad) beans
500 ml (2 cups) vegetable stock
750 ml (3 cups) water
2 onions, roughly chopped into
   wedges
5 garlic cloves, sliced
2 teaspoons pepper
2 teaspoons salt
2 teaspoons ground cumin
Large bunch of cilantro, stems
   removed and roughly chopped
   (about 3 cups)
Large bunch of parsley, stems
   removed and roughly chopped
   (about 1 cup)
Large bunch of dill, roughly
   chopped (about 1 ½ cups)
2 tablespoons dried mint
2 tablespoons white or apple
   cider vinegar

For the fried onion topping:
2 onions, diced
4 tablespoons coconut oil
4 garlic cloves, minced
1 tablespoon ground coriander

Time: 60 minutes + 2 or more hours soaking time for the beans

First, rinse the beans under cold water, cover with lukewarm water, and soak 2 hours or overnight.

Drain and rinse the beans and put them in a large pan. Add the stock and the water, the onions and garlic, and the cumin, salt, and pepper.

Bring to the boil, then lower the heat and let simmer, covered, for 45 minutes. You will see the beans becoming soft and tender when you stir the mix. After about 30–35 minutes, stir in the chopped greens and dried mint, making sure all is well combined.

While the beans cook, use a large pan to shallow-fry the diced onions in the coconut oil until light gold in color. Add the minced garlic and ground coriander and fry for another 5 minutes, or until the onions turn darker. Make sure to stand by the pan at all times as the onions can burn in a second.

Use a stick blender or food processor to whizz the beans until you have the consistency of a creamy soup. Return the beans to the heat, stir in half of the fried onions and most of the oil, then, just before you turn off the heat, drizzle in the vinegar and stir one last time.

Let it cool a little; as it does so, it will thicken to the consistency of a dip. Just before serving, garnish with the rest of the fried onions.

Egyptian Falafel with Green Onion and Tomato

 vegan   protein-packed   gluten-free

The most acclaimed Middle Eastern street food is the falafel, wholesome, vegan, and addictively tasty, with its fluffy center in a crispy shell. This is our take on the Egyptian recipe, in which fava beans are used. Traditionally, falafels are deep-fried, but we bake ours to cut down on the fat content. Drizzle with a thinned tahini sauce or serve with a tomato, cucumber, and onion salad.

Makes: about 16 pieces

250 g (8 oz) dried split fava (broad) beans
2 onions, quartered
Bunch of parsley, stems removed
Bunch of cilantro, stems removed
Small bunch of dill
Small bunch of mint, stems removed
2 leeks, roughly chopped
3 garlic cloves
1 teaspoon ground cumin
2 teaspoons salt
1 teaspoon pepper
1 teaspoon baking soda
3 green onions, finely chopped
1 tomato, deseeded and diced
Olive oil, for brushing
2–3 tablespoons sesame seeds

Time: 40 minutes + soaking time for the beans

Rinse the beans well under cold running water and place in a large bowl. Fill the bowl with fresh lukewarm water and let the beans soak for at least 2 hours or ideally overnight. You will need to top up the water at least once.

Bring a small pan of water to the boil and simmer the onions for about 15 minutes. Lift them out and whizz briefly in a food processor, then tip them into a sieve over a bowl and, with a spoon, press out as much of the liquid as you can. It's this onion liquor from the bowl that you need for the recipe.

Now, preheat the oven to 180°C (350°F/Gas mark 4).

Put all the green herbs in a food processor and pulse until finely chopped. Add the leeks and garlic, pulsing until minced.

Drain the beans and add them to the food processor along with the onion liquor. Add the cumin, the baking soda, and salt and pepper. Pulse until completely combined into a fluffy, bright green dough. Stop the food processor a couple of times to scrape the sides down and fluff up the batter.

Fold in the chopped green onions and diced tomatoes.

Line an oven tray with baking parchment and brush it generously with olive oil.

With your hands, form the mixture into about 16 small balls, then flatten them slightly to make a small patty shape. Brush both sides with olive oil generously, place on the oven tray, then sprinkle sesame seeds on top.

Bake the falafel in the middle of the oven for about 25 minutes, turning them halfway through, until they are crispy on the outside and fluffy and cooked-through inside.

When they're done, wait for a couple of minutes before lifting the falafels from the baking parchment, then serve straightaway.

Baked Yellow Lentil Falafel

طعمية عدس أصفر مخبوزة

 vegan   protein-packed   gluten-free

While Levantine cuisine introduced the world to chickpea-based falafel, this is the Moroccan take on this yummy, crispy Middle Eastern specialty. Yellow or red lentil falafels have a wonderfully crunchy shell even when baked rather than deep-fried, and they're more tender on the inside than chickpea falafels, which can be grainy. Amazingly, you don't need to precook the lentils—soaking alone will make them tender enough to grind in a food processor to a fine texture, perfect for falafel dough.

To make a complete meal of these nutritious falafel, serve them with something contrastingly soft and unctuous, such as roasted eggplant, and perhaps a green salad.

Makes: about 20 pieces

400 g (14 oz) yellow lentils (about 2 cups)
1 onion, cut into chunks
3 garlic cloves
Small bunch of cilantro, stalks removed and finely chopped (about ½ cup)
Small bunch of parsley, stalks removed and finely chopped (about ½ cup)
1 tablespoon olive oil (and more for brushing)
2 teaspoons ground cumin
½ teaspoon baking soda
1 egg
Salt and pepper
4 tablespoons black seeds (also known as nigella seeds)

Time: 40 minutes + 2 hours soaking time

Wash the lentils, then soak them in cold water for about 2 hours (or overnight).

When you're ready to cook, put the onion and garlic in a food processor and pulse until finely chopped. Add the cilantro, cumin, and baking soda and pulse again. Transfer the mix to a medium-sized mixing bowl and set aside.

Preheat the oven to 180°C (350°F/Gas mark 4). Line an oven tray with baking parchment and brush the paper generously with olive oil.

Rinse the lentils and place them in the food processor with the olive oil. Pulse to grind them to a smooth paste and then add to the onion mix.

Crack the egg over the mixture and season with salt and pepper. Use your hands to combine everything together. You need to be able to form it into a ball that will hold its shape, so if it seems too crumbly, add a couple of tablespoons of hot water. Then form the mixture into about 20 small patty shapes or cylinders, brush them with olive oil, and place them on the oven tray.

Sprinkle the black seeds over the falafels, then bake them in the oven for about 20 minutes, turning them halfway through. Serve warm.

Roasted Eggplants with Tahini and Pomegranate Molasses Dressing

 vegan   paleo   🌾 gluten-free

Eggplants are a heavenly ingredient, a mainstay of the healthy Mediterranean diet and a staple of Middle Eastern cuisine. For a light dish in which you can really taste the essence of eggplant, we simply roast them in olive oil and combine them with arugula, a tahini dressing, and one of our favorite ingredients, sweet-sharp pomegranate molasses. It's a recipe that just impresses in any setting.

Makes: mezze for 4

2 large eggplants
Large bunch of arugula (about 2 cups), torn and stems removed
2 tablespoons olive oil
Salt and pepper

For the tahini dressing:
4 tablespoons tahini paste
2 garlic cloves, minced
Juice of 1 large lime
½ teaspoon ground coriander
¼ teaspoon ground cumin
Salt and pepper

To garnish:
Handful of pomegranate seeds
2 tablespoons pomegranate molasses
2 tablespoons pine nuts, toasted (optional)

Time: 45 minutes

Preheat the oven to 180°C (350°F/Gas mark 4). Line an oven tray with baking parchment.

Slice the eggplants into thin rounds, brush them lightly on both sides with 1 tablespoon of the olive oil, and lay them carefully next to each other in one layer on the oven tray. Place in the middle of the oven for 30 minutes until fully cooked, turning halfway through.

While the eggplant slices roast, put all of the ingredients for the dressing along with about 4 ¼ cups lukewarm water into a medium bowl and mix to combine. If the dressing is too thick for your liking, you can mix in a little water.

When the eggplants cool, arrange them next to each other on a plate, drizzle with tahini mix, and then lay arugula leaves on top. Season with salt and pepper, drizzle olive oil, and pomegranate molasses. You can garnish with a handful of fresh pomegranate seeds and toasted pine nuts.

Smoked Eggplant Dip

 بابا غنوج مدخن

 vegan   paleo   gluten-free

This recipe is extra-simple; you don't need to prepare the eggplants or even brush them with olive oil. You just place them under the grill and turn them occasionally, enjoying the wonderful aroma as they cook, until they emerge, soft and caramelized and so easy to peel. In this recipe, which is similar to the popular el-raheb, a Lebanese/Syrian mashed eggplant salad, the eggplant is combined with other vegetables to make a perfect, filling snack, appetizer, or even breakfast dish. You can prepare bigger batches for gatherings and serve with crackers or crudités.

Makes: mezze for 4

1 eggplant
1 red bell pepper, diced
1 small tomato, deseeded and diced
2 green onions, finely chopped
3 tablespoons capers
1 tablespoon fresh thyme leaves, finely chopped
Juice of 1 lime
1 tablespoon extra-virgin olive oil, plus a drizzle to garnish
2 garlic cloves, minced
Salt and pepper
1 tablespoon black seeds (also known as nigella seeds), to garnish

Time: 40 minutes

Preheat the grill. Line a grill pan or oven tray with baking parchment.

Pierce the eggplant with a fork in several places all around and place it on the tray. Grill for 30 minutes or until blackened, turning frequently. Let it cool, then peel and finely chop it.

To a medium bowl, add the chopped eggplant, red pepper and tomato, green onions, capers, thyme, lime juice, olive oil, garlic, and salt and pepper. Mix to combine, then sprinkle the sesame seeds on top and drizzle over a little more olive oil.

Green 'Eggah

 protein-packed

A traditional Egyptian baked omelet, 'eggah is the perfect brunch dish when there are several mouths to feed. We make ours with onions and leeks and plenty of fresh herbs, but you can include almost anything—green peppers, tomatoes, and cheese are popular additions. 'Eggah is customarily prepared with potatoes and white flour to give it a fluffy thickness (almost like a moist cake), but we use quinoa to boost the protein content already supplied by the eggs and lower the gluten content, making this a perfect post-workout morning meal. Enjoy with a side salad or some crackers.

Makes: 6–8 slices

2 tablespoons coconut oil
2 onions, diced
2 leeks, finely chopped
Salt
10 eggs
Pepper
1 ½ teaspoons ground cumin
Bunch of dill, finely chopped
  (about 1 cup)
Bunch of cilantro, stems removed
  and finely chopped (about 1
  cup)
Bunch of parsley, stems removed
  and finely chopped (about 1
  cup)
Handful of mint, stems removed
  and finely chopped (about 2
  tablespoons)
Drop of olive oil and more for
  brushing
2 tablespoons water
¼ cup (60 ml) almond or oat milk
100 g (3 ½ oz) cooked quinoa
  (about ½ cup)

Time: 45 minutes

Preheat the oven to 180°C (350°F/Gas mark 4).

In a large pan over a low to medium heat, melt the coconut oil and sauté the onions and leeks gently until softened. Season with salt and stir occasionally, until cooked but not colored (about 8 minutes), and set aside to cool.

Crack the eggs into a large bowl, season with pepper and add the cumin. Whisk together well, then add all the chopped herbs and a drop of olive oil (which helps give some fluffiness to the dish). The texture will become thicker, so add the water and milk and whisk until well combined. Add the cooked and cooled quinoa, leeks, and onions.

Brush a round oven dish with olive oil and pour in the egg mixture making sure the solid ingredients are equally spread. Place in the middle of the oven for about 25–30 minutes until the eggs are cooked through, and serve immediately.

Mediterranean Omelet
with Goat's Milk Feta

بيض بالزيتون وجبنة الماعز

⚕ protein-packed

A morning run or workout will fly by when you have this scrumptious breakfast omelet to look forward to. The combination of the eggs with the Mediterranean vegetables and cheese, fragrant with mood-boosting thyme, is filling enough with no need for bread, giving you the restorative protein and nutrients you need for the day without weighing you down with carbs. Serve it with some peppery arugula for a complete meal.

Makes: 3–4 servings

2 tablespoons coconut oil
1 red onion, thinly sliced
1 small tomato, deseeded and
    diced
Handful of pitted black olives,
    sliced
6 eggs
60 ml (¼ cup) almond milk
Drop of olive oil
1 tablespoon fresh thyme leaves
Salt and pepper
40 g (2 oz) goat's milk feta

Time: 15 minutes

Heat the coconut oil in a large frying pan over a medium heat. Add the onions and let them cook for a couple of minutes before adding the tomato and black olives.

As the vegetables cook, beat the eggs, almond milk, and olive oil together in a medium bowl. Add the thyme and season generously with salt and pepper.

As the veggies gain some color, spread them out evenly in the pan then pour the egg mixture over them. You won't need to flip the omelet if you keep drawing in the cooked sides to allow the runny egg to reach the pan. When it is almost cooked, crumble over the feta and sprinkle over a few more thyme leaves, if desired. It should take about 8 minutes for the omelet to be ready to serve.

Fried Eggs with Dates

بيض بالعجوة

(⚭) protein-packed

This is a delicious breakfast dish that traditionally uses either *rottab* (fresh dates) or *'agwa*, a thick date paste often used to stuff pastries. Its sweet-and-savory flavor profile is not that common in Middle Eastern cuisine, but for us it's such a familiar one; we were raised eating this dish for the Ramadan predawn meal, before the day's fasting began. Full of protein, fiber, and sugars for energy, it's both nutritious and filling, perfect before a long day. You can cook it in ghee instead of coconut oil for a more traditional flavor.

Makes: 2 servings

2 tablespoons coconut oil
1 green onion, finely chopped
4 Medjoul or fresh black dates
3 eggs
Salt and pepper

Time: 10 minutes

Heat the coconut oil in a medium frying pan and sauté the chopped green onion for a couple of minutes.

Pit the dates and slice each into 4 pieces, add them to the pan, and sauté for a couple more minutes. Spread the dates and onion out evenly in the pan. Crack the eggs straight into the pan and let them cook for about 5 minutes, until the whites are firm. Season with salt and pepper and serve with some crusty bread.

Vegetable-filled Egg Shakshouka

شكشوكة البيض والخضار

 paleo   protein-packed

This is a popular breakfast dish in Egypt, Palestine, and other Mediterranean Arab countries with endless variations, but onions, tomatoes, and fried eggs are the constants. When you add the eggs, make sure that they touch the bottom of the pan so that the egg white will cook quickly enough for the yolks to stay runny and delicious.

You could also add some cooked chickpeas with the tomatoes for a more filling dish, or, right at the end, crumble over some goat's milk cheese for an extra kick.

Makes: 4–6 servings

2 tablespoons olive oil
1 large onion, thinly sliced
2 garlic cloves, minced
2 yellow bell peppers, cut into thin strips
2 red bell peppers, cut into thin strips
5 tomatoes, peeled and diced, with all their juice
½ teaspoon ground cumin
Salt and pepper
Pinch of cinnamon
6 eggs
Handful of parsley, stems removed and finely chopped (about 2 tablespoons)
1 tablespoon dried mint powder (optional)

Time: 20 minutes

Heat the olive oil in a large frying pan and add the onions followed by the garlic. Sauté the onions until cooked through (about 7 minutes).

Add the sliced peppers, cumin, and salt and pepper. Let the vegetables cook for a couple of minutes, stirring occasionally.

Add the tomatoes and the cinnamon. Lower the heat and simmer for about 7 minutes before adding the eggs.

To add the eggs, use the back of your wooden spoon to clear six round wells in the mixture, and crack an egg into each. Grind a little salt and pepper over the eggs, and let them cook for another 5 minutes, until the whites are cooked but the yolks are still shiny and runny. Before taking it off the heat, sprinkle over the parsley and mint powder.

White Bean and Sun-dried Tomato Dip

 vegan 　 protein-packed

This recipe is as easy as most healthy dips and sandwich fillers. It's all about preparing the ingredients (mainly chopping), then letting your food processor work its magic! This dip is creamy, full of flavor, filling, and oh, so comforting. You can serve it with crudités at a gathering or use it to fill buns for your lunchbox. If you're using sun-dried tomatoes bottled in oil, you can use that oil instead of the olive oil in the recipe. It will work just as well to achieve a smooth texture, while adding even more flavor.

Makes: a dip for 6–8

Handful of parsley, stems removed and roughly chopped (3 tablespoons)
1 tablespoon fresh thyme leaves
2 green onions, chopped
3 garlic cloves
150 g (5 oz) sun-dried tomatoes, thinly sliced
Juice of 1 lime
Salt and pepper
500 g (1 lb 2 oz) cooked butter beans
2 tablespoons olive oil

Time: 10 minutes

Put the roughly chopped parsley, thyme, garlic, and green onions into a full-sized food processor, and pulse until finely chopped.

Add the sun-dried tomatoes, lime juice, and salt and pepper, then the beans and pulse, pausing occasionally to scrape down the sides of the bowl, until well combined.

Add the olive oil and pulse until everything is smooth and fully integrated.

Before serving, adjust the seasoning if required and, if you think it needs it, add an extra squeeze of lime juice.

Smoked Herring with Tahini and Capers

 gluten-free   paleo   protein-packed

Renga is a type of salted and smoked herring that, in our part of the world, is traditionally eaten at the Easter-time festival of Sham el-Nessim. At its simplest it's served with green onion and a squeeze of lime juice, but there are a multitude of family recipes that are treasured and passed down the generations. This is our "party" herring dish, and it's a real crowd-pleaser; we serve it with sliced carrot and celery crudités, and it always goes down well.

Smoked herring in one form or another is found almost all over the world, and most will suit this dish perfectly. There are good bottled and canned brands, too—just be sure not to pick up pickled herrings, as the vinegar will overpower and ruin the dish.

Makes: a dip for 6-8

175 g (6 oz) tahini paste (about ¾ cup)
½ teaspoon ground cumin
½ teaspoon ground coriander
Salt and pepper
3 limes, 2 of them juiced
60 ml (¼ cup) lukewarm water
300 g (10 ½ oz) smoked herring fillets
1 small red onion, thinly sliced
2 tablespoons capers

Time: 10 minutes

In a medium bowl, mix the tahini with the cumin and coriander, lime juice, and water, and season with salt and pepper. Stir well to combine.

Slice the herring fillets into thin strips and stir them into the tahini mix. If you feel the consistency is too lumpy for a dip, put it in a food processor, but only for a couple of pulses (you don't want it to be creamy-smooth).

Mix in the thinly sliced red onions, and transfer to a serving bowl. Give it a final squeeze of the remaining lime, then garnish with the capers and a grinding of black pepper.

Breakfast & Mezze   45

Bottarga Salad

 gluten-free 　　🚫 paleo 　　🥤 protein-packed

Bottarga is an age-old delicacy common to most Mediterranean countries, especially North Africa and Italy. This salted, pressed, and sun-dried fish roe, usually from grey mullet, comes as a solid, reddish or coral-colored block that is traditionally shaved or very thinly sliced and eaten on crusty bread with red or green onions, olive oil or butter, and lots of lime juice. Being a fishy by-product, bottarga is rich in omega-3 fatty acids and zinc, both essential nutrients with a range of health benefits. Here we create a simple salad from this gorgeous ingredient that highlights all its savory intensity. It makes an elegant appetizer or, with some gluten-free crackers, a nutritious light lunch.

Makes: 2–4 servings

Around 150 g (6 oz) bottarga, thinly sliced
Juice of 2 limes
2 cups of arugula, roughly torn
60 ml (¼ cup) olive oil
Salt
1 teaspoon black pepper
½ red onion, thinly sliced
3 garlic cloves, thinly sliced

Time: 10 minutes

In a shallow salad bowl, place arugula leaves. Season lightly with salt, and drizzle over half of the olive oil. Scatter over the bottarga slices, then sprinkle over the lime juice and black pepper.

Add the onion and garlic, drizzle the rest of the olive oil on top, and use your hands or salad servers to toss all the ingredients gently together.

Spicy Crispy Chickpeas

⊘ vegan   ✿ gluten-free   ⚕ protein-packed

These tasty little morsels are positively addictive. The secret of success with this recipe (which otherwise couldn't be easier) is to make sure the cooked chickpeas are completely dry before you begin. If you're using canned chickpeas, rinse them really thoroughly then dry them on a clean dish towel.

In the unlikely event that there are any leftovers, they'll keep in an airtight container for around three days. Pop them in a hot oven for a couple of minutes before serving to revive their freshness. You can also sprinkle these crispy balls over your salads.

Makes: a generous mezze dish

500 g (1 lb 2 oz) cooked
   chickpeas (see Hummus
   on page 19 for cooking
   instructions)
2 tablespoons olive oil
1 teaspoon salt
½ teaspoon garlic powder
½ teaspoon ground cumin
½ teaspoon ground coriander
½ teaspoon paprika
Pinch of chili powder (optional)
Zest of ½ lime

Time: 40 minutes

Preheat the oven to 200°C (400°F/Gas mark 6). Line an oven tray with baking parchment.

Spread the chickpeas out on the oven tray and place in the oven for about 10 minutes before seasoning.

In a small bowl, mix the olive oil with the salt and all the spices. When the 10 minutes are up, take the tray out of the oven, sprinkle the olive oil mix over the chickpeas and muddle them around a little to make sure they are all well coated. Return to the oven for another 20–25 minutes, giving the tray a shake every few minutes to make sure the chickpeas crisp up on all sides. Sprinkle lime zest and serve straightaway.

Gluten-free Granola Squares with Apricots and Prunes

 vegan   protein-packed   gluten-free

So many granola bar recipes are out there that it's about time we had one that celebrates Middle Eastern dried fruits like apricots and prunes, and all the health benefits they bring. Muslims set great store by dried fruits during Ramadan: their natural sugars and fiber provide energy during long fasting days, and they're great for relieving constipation caused by the change in eating patterns, not to mention dehydration during the day.

This nourishing mix is gluten-free and lightly sweetened with raw honey (vegans could substitute molasses). You could use it to replace breakfast (or indeed any other meal) and it's a wholesome treat to pop in a lunchbox.

Makes: 9 pieces

250 g (9 oz) almonds (about 1 cup), preferably peeled
4 tablespoons flax seeds
4 tablespoons sesame seeds
50 g (1 ½ oz) coconut flakes (about ½ cup), plus 2 tablespoons to garnish (optional)
40 g (1 ½ oz) sunflower seeds (about ¼ cup)
170 g (6 oz) dried apricots, (about 1 cup), roughly chopped
100 g (3 ½ oz) prunes (about ½ cup), pitted and roughly chopped
½ teaspoon cinnamon (optional)
4 tablespoons almond butter
4 tablespoons raw honey

Time: 30 minutes

Preheat the oven to 200°C (400°F/Gas Mark 6) and line a rectangular or square 20-by-20-cm (8-by-8-inch) oven tray with baking parchment. (A drop of coconut oil brushed on the underside of the paper will make it adhere neatly to the tray.)

In a food processor or grinder, pulse the almonds and flax seeds into a rough powder.

In a dry skillet over a medium heat, toast the sesame, sunflower seeds, and coconut for a couple of minutes, until golden and fragrant. Set aside.

Put the chopped apricots and prunes into a medium bowl and add the almond-flax powder, the toasted seeds and coconut, and (if using) the cinnamon, and stir everything together well to ensure you have an even mixture. Now add the almond butter and honey, folding them in with a spatula until everything is well combined together.

Spoon the mixture onto the oven tray, distributing it evenly. Use your hands to press it down to form an even layer, 1–1.5cm (about ½ in) deep.

Place in the middle of the oven for 15 minutes. If you like, after 10 minutes in the oven, sprinkle 2 tablespoons coconut over the granola and return it to the oven for the last 5 minutes, or until the coconut is toasted. Let it cool for 10 minutes before you slice it into squares. Keep it in an airtight container for up to 4 days.

Cinnamon and Sea-salt Almond Butter

 vegan   paleo   protein-packed

Almonds not only contain lots of calcium, but also confer cardiovascular benefits because of their healthy fats: the type that improve blood cholesterol levels and boost energy. They're full of fiber too. So a couple of tablespoons of almond butter a day—with your oats, spread on gluten-free crackers, or used as a dip for fresh fruits—will keep you feeling full as well as feeling well! Turning nuts into butter isn't the easiest job for a food processor, and this is one of those occasions when investing in good quality, robust kitchen equipment really pays off.

Makes: 1 medium jar

500 g (1 lb 1 oz) almonds, unpeeled (about 2 cups)
2 teaspoons cinnamon
1 teaspoon salt
1–2 tablespoons coconut oil (optional)

Time: 45 minutes

Preheat the oven to 180°C (350°F/Gas mark 4) and line a large oven tray with baking parchment. Spread the almonds out on the tray and sprinkle with the cinnamon and salt. Roast for 20 minutes, or until lightly toasted but not darkened. Remove from the oven and let them cool for 15 minutes.

Scrape the almonds and all the bits and pieces of cinnamon and salt into a sturdy food processor or grinder and blitz them to a cream. This will take at least 5–10 minutes: you will have to pulse then stop, to scrape down the sides of the bowl, then pulse again.

If it creams but the texture is not as smooth as you want it to be, keep going, and try adding coconut oil little by little until you achieve a texture you like. Stored in a sterilized jar, it will keep for up to a month.

Homemade Strawberry Jam

مربّى الفراولة

 paleo

Jams are very popular in the Middle East, as sandwich fillers or as an accompaniment to cake or biscuits. We are sweet-toothed people and like to be sure we have a supply always to hand in the pantry or fridge. The beauty of this jam is not only that it needs no refined sugar to be delicious, but also that it only takes a few minutes to make a jar that will see you through the week. (Yes, it takes takes 7 minutes to cook and keeps up to 7 days in the fridge!) The minimal cooking time preserves all the color and nutrients in the fruits, and adding superfood chia seeds has got to be the easiest "jamming" technique ever. It works with all sorts of fruits, so you can follow the seasons with different flavors. Although this is a fresh jam, not destined for a long life, you should still sterilize the jar before storing it.

Makes: 1 medium jar

500 g (1 lb 2oz) strawberries
Juice of 1 lime
2 tablespoons raw honey
Pinch of salt
3 tablespoons chia seeds

Time: 15 minutes

Put the strawberries into a medium pan over a low to medium heat. They will start to soften and release their juices quickly. Add the lime juice and stir them occasionally while they cook, for about 7 minutes.

Remove from the heat, and add the honey, salt, and chia seeds. Stir slowly to combine until the chia seeds have soaked up the fruit juices and the jam has thickened.

Tip the mixture slowly into a sterilized glass jar, let it cool for a couple of minutes, then close tightly and pop it in the fridge.

Soups & Stews الشوربة

Bone Broth

شوربة كوارع

 gluten-free   paleo   protein-packed

A savory broth made from simmering animal bones or meat scraps with vegetables, herbs, and spices forms the base for many Middle Eastern soups, sauces, and stews. A cup of hot bone broth just by itself also makes a calcium-rich, nourishing pick-me-up with many health benefits.

You can make this broth in a large slow cooker (it'll take 24 hours on a low setting), but you must still follow the first step to remove impurities that rise to the top as scum.

Most butchers will be happy to give you some beef bones; alternatively, use a cooked chicken carcass. Or, if you're meat-free, just the vegetables, flavorings, and herbs alone will make a flavorful, nutritious veggie stock for soups and casseroles.

Makes: around 1 liter (4 cups or 1 quart)

1 kg (2.2 lb) beef shin bones, or similar
3 large carrots, peeled and cut into chunks
4 celery stalks, sliced
1 large onion, quartered
1 whole garlic bulb, cloves separated and peeled
2 tablespoons coconut oil
1 tablespoon apple cider vinegar
5 cm (2 in) piece of ginger, peeled and sliced
1 bunch parsley
2 bay leaves
10 peppercorns
1 cinnamon stick
5 cardamom pods
4 granules mastic
8 cups water, or enough to cover
Salt to taste

Time: 2 hours +

Rinse the bones under cold running water, then place them in a large pan of cold water and heat until froth starts to float to the top. Remove the bones, dump the water, and clean out the pot.

Put the bones back in the pot, together with all the other ingredients, and cover with water.

Cover and bring to a slow simmer for at least 2 hours. The broth will get richer and more flavorful the longer you let it simmer.

Strain the broth from the bones and vegetables, and discard these.

Season with salt to taste. It will last one week in the fridge and up to a month in the freezer.

Lentil and Vegetable Soup

 gluten-free   (∅) vegan   (⊥) protein-packed

A traditional dish in most Arab countries, this soup is filling, comforting and just pleases everyone. If you're a meat-eater, you can of course use bone broth or chicken stock as the base, but if you need to keep it vegan and don't have any ready-made vegetable stock, just use water and add a cardamom pod and a bay leaf for an extra flavor twist.

Middle Eastern lentil soup is traditionally whizzed into a creamy consistency. In this recipe, however, we leave the diced vegetables cooked in this light broth and add baby spinach to it at the end for a further kick.

Makes: 4–5 servings

2 tablespoons olive oil
3 green onions, finely chopped
2 carrots, diced
3 garlic cloves, minced
1 teaspoon ground cumin
½ teaspoon paprika
400 g (14 oz) yellow lentils (about 2 cups)
3 tomatoes, diced
1 liter (4 cups) vegetable stock
Salt and pepper
Handful of baby spinach leaves, sliced

Time: 30 minutes

Heat the olive oil in a deep pan and sauté the green onions, carrots, and garlic for a few minutes. Sprinkle in the cumin, paprika, and salt and pepper to taste, and stir.

Rinse the lentils in a sieve and drain, then add the lentils and the tomatoes to the pan and stir them in.

Add the stock and bring to the boil, then cover, lower the heat, and let simmer for 20 minutes, until the lentils and vegetables are cooked through. Serve in large bowls, sprinkled with the sliced baby spinach.

Moroccan Chickpea Soup

شوربة حمص مغربية

⊘ vegan   ✻ gluten-free   ⚕ protein-packed

Inspired by the Egyptian *hallabessa*, a hot, spicy chickpea drink sometimes called *hummus el-sham*, this soup is full of delicious spicy flavors without needing any homemade broth or stock. It is also high on non-animal protein and other nutritious ingredients, and super filling for lunch or dinner. You can adjust the quantity of chili in the recipe to suit the level of heat you like. This is a great way to use up a cup of leftover cooked chickpeas in the refrigerator; if starting with raw chickpeas, you'll need to soak them overnight and then preboil for 60 minutes before starting the soup.

Makes: 4–5 servings

2 tablespoons olive oil
1 large onion, diced
5 garlic cloves, minced
½ –1 chili pepper, finely diced
4 tomatoes, finely chopped
1 teaspoon turmeric
1 teaspoon paprika
Salt and pepper
170 g (6 oz) cooked chickpeas
   (about 1 cup) (see Hummus
   on page 19 for cooking
   instructions)
Juice of 1 lime
Handful of cilantro, chopped, to
   garnish

Time: 45 minutes

Heat the olive oil in a deep pan and sauté the onions, garlic, and chili until just golden (about 8 minutes). Add the tomatoes, spices, and salt and pepper, and stir for a couple of minutes.

Add about 4 cups hot water and stir to combine. Add the chickpeas, then cover and let the soup simmer for 20 minutes, or until the chickpeas are meltingly soft. Serve warm, adding a sprinkle of lime juice and chopped cilantro to each bowl.

Cauliflower, Garlic, and Almond Soup

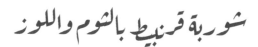

 paleo   gluten-free

Creamy and rich, with warming, nutty flavors, this luscious soup is a perfect family comfort food, but equally good as an elegant appetizer. While the recipe isn't traditionally Middle Eastern, it's our modern take on some typical, commonly used ingredients. It's a surprise it wasn't invented here long ago.

Makes: 5 servings

3 large whole bulbs of garlic
1 large yellow onion, minced
2 tablespoons coconut oil, melted, or olive oil
About half a medium cauliflower, cut into florets (about 2 cups)
1 liter (4 cups) chicken stock
250 ml (1 cup) almond milk
100 g (4 oz) peeled almonds
1 pinch nutmeg
Salt and pepper
Handful of cilantro, finely chopped, to garnish

Time: 60 minutes

Preheat the oven to 170°C (325°F/Gas mark 3). Cut across the top of the garlic bulbs, then place them on the chopping board and press down on them with the palm of your hand over the flat of a knife to splay out the cloves a little. Place them on an oven tray and roast for 25–30 minutes.

While the garlic roasts, heat the oil in a deep pan on a low to medium heat, and sauté the onion until translucent (about 7 minutes). Add the cauliflower florets and stir to combine.

Add the chicken stock, nutmeg, and salt and pepper to taste, and bring to the boil, then cover, lower the heat, and simmer gently for around 15 minutes.

In a dry skillet, toast the almonds for a couple of minutes.

Peel the garlic cloves (roasting makes this so easy – the skin will just fall off). Add the garlic, toasted almonds, and almond milk to the soup.

Blend the soup to a creamy texture, and adjust the seasoning if necessary. Serve garnished with the chopped cilantro.

Carrot and Ginger Soup

شوربة جزر بالجنزبيل

 vegan   gluten-free

This is one of the soups we cook most often at home. It's so easy and quick, and the spices make it delicious without the need for stock. Coconut oil and ginger work really well with carrots and you can, if you like, include coconut (or almond) milk to make it even creamier without adding any dairy or starch. With its healthy ingredients and cleansing spices, this soup could easily form part of a detox plan.

You can keep it refrigerated for up to 4 days if you're not using coconut or almond milk, otherwise two days.

Makes: 4 generous servings

2 tablespoons coconut oil
1 onion, diced
3 garlic cloves, minced
5 cm (2 in) piece of fresh ginger, grated
1 teaspoon ground cumin
1 teaspoon cinnamon
2 cardamom pods
2 bay leaves
2 cloves
1 kg (2 ¼ lb) carrots, grated
Salt and pepper
1250 ml (5-6 cups) hot water
Juice of 2 limes
2 tablespoons pumpkin seeds
125 ml (½ cup) coconut milk or almond milk (optional)

Time: 30 minutes

You need a large soup pan for this one. First, melt the coconut oil and sauté the diced onion for about 5 minutes. Add the garlic, ginger, and all the spices, and stir and sauté for a couple more minutes.

Add the grated carrot, and some salt and pepper. Stir until the carrot is softened and wilted down, then add 5 cups hot water, cover, and bring to a simmer for about 10 minutes.

While the soup simmers, toast the pumpkin seeds in a dry skillet over a medium heat for a couple of minutes. Set aside.

Add the lime juice to the soup, then discard the bay leaves, cardamom, and cloves.

Blend the soup to a smooth texture and adjust the seasoning to taste. If you want that extra creaminess, return it to the stove and drizzle in the coconut or almond milk, and stir over a medium heat for a couple more minutes.

Serve hot, with the toasted seeds sprinkled on top.

Creamy Broccoli and Arugula Soup

 vegan   gluten-free

This soup was inspired a few years back by Gwyneth Paltrow's *It's All Good* collection of clean, good-for-you recipes. Our version incorporates local spices that add warming, Middle Eastern flavors, and we also use the broccoli stem as well as the florets to achieve a more substantial, filling soup without adding any potatoes or cream.

One of the flavorings we use here is mastic, which may be unfamiliar to some. It's a gum collected from a species of tree in the cashew family that is sold as small, translucent granules often called pearls. The flavor is distinctive: resiny, almost piney, and redolent of sunbaked hillsides. It's very strong, so use it sparingly.

Makes: 4 generous servings

2 tablespoons olive oil
1 large onion, diced
2 garlic cloves, minced
2 granules mastic
1250 ml (5-6 cups) hot water
1 medium head broccoli
2 pods cardamom
2 bay leaves
2 handfuls arugula
Salt and pepper
2 tablespoons flax seeds
   (optional)

Time: 30 minutes

Cut the florets from the broccoli head, and then chop the stem, discarding any woody part at the base.

In a large pan, heat the olive oil and sauté the onions, garlic, and mastic for a few minutes until the onions are translucent.

Stir in the broccoli florets and chopped stem, then add the hot water, bay leaves, and cardamom. Bring to the boil, then lower the heat, cover, and simmer for about 15 minutes, until the broccoli is softened. Add the arugula and stir for a couple more minutes, then take the pan off the heat.

Remove the cardamom and bay leaves, then blend the soup to a creamy texture. Season with salt and pepper to taste.

In a dry skillet, toast the flax seeds over a medium heat for a couple of minutes, shaking the pan continuously. Serve the soup hot, with a sprinkling of flax seeds on top for some crunch.

Spiced Pumpkin Soup

شوربة قرع بالبهارات

vegan   paleo   protein-packed

Middle Eastern infusions work so well to lift the flavor of lightly sweet pumpkin in this warming, comforting soup. You can blend all of the finished soup until smooth and creamy, or just half to leave some chunks for texture.

Makes: 6 servings

2 tablespoons coconut oil
3 green onions, chopped + extra to garnish
2 stalks celery, chopped
2 cloves garlic, minced
1 chili pepper, seeds removed and finely chopped (optional)
2 teaspoons turmeric
Pinch of ground nutmeg
2 carrots, roughly chopped
600 g (1 lb 5 oz) fresh pumpkin, peeled, deseeded, and cut into chunks
2 bay leaves
3 sprigs fresh thyme
1000–1250 ml (4–5 cups) of water, or enough to cover
Salt and pepper
Handful of cilantro, chopped, to garnish

Time: 45 minutes

In a large pan on medium heat, melt the coconut oil and sauté the green onions, celery, garlic, and chili (if using) for a few minutes until softened.

Stir in the turmeric and nutmeg then add the carrot, pumpkin, bay leaves, thyme, and water. Bring to the boil, then reduce the heat, cover, and simmer for about 40 minutes, until the pumpkin is very tender. Season generously with salt and pepper.

When the soup is ready, blend to the desired texture, and serve hot, garnished with chopped green onions and cilantro.

Creamy Chestnut Soup

 شوربة الكستناء

 paleo   gluten-free   ⚕ protein-packed

Roasted chestnuts are a simple, popular snack in the cooler Middle Eastern countries. This luscious soup celebrates the nuttiness and creaminess of this low-fat yet protein-packed nut. Because you roast the chestnuts first, the soup itself is quick to cook, giving it a freshness to balance the richness, and the addition of fresh thyme right at the end of cooking gives a lovely little lift of fragrance.

Makes: 4–5 servings

500–700 g (18–24 oz) chestnuts in their shells (about 2 cups when peeled)
2 tablespoons olive oil
1 onion, finely chopped
750 ml (3 cups) bone or chicken broth (see Bone Broth on page 59)
250 ml (1 cup) almond milk
3 garlic cloves, minced
1 ½ tablespoons chopped fresh thyme
Salt and pepper

Time: 15 minutes + 1 hour to roast the chestnuts

Preheat the oven to 150°C (300°F/Gas mark 2).

Wipe the chestnuts clean and, with a small sharp knife, make a cross-cut on the flat surface of each. Lay them cut side up on an oven tray, and put in the oven to roast for 50–60 minutes. Peel the cooked chestnuts once they are cool enough to handle.

Heat the olive oil in a deep pan on low to medium heat, and sauté the onions gently until translucent (about 7 minutes). Add the peeled chestnuts and cook, stirring, for another minute.

Add the broth, almond milk, and garlic. Bring to the boil, then lower the heat and simmer for about 5 minutes, stirring occasionally.

Add the chopped thyme, then blend until smooth and creamy. Season with salt and pepper to taste, and serve warm.

Salads, Pulses, & Grains

الس‍‍طات والبقوليات

Traditional Tomato and Onion Salad

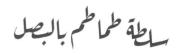

 vegan   paleo   ⊛ gluten-free

Tomatoes are used in so many Middle Eastern dishes, especially in those countries that border the Mediterranean. This salad celebrates the vibrancy of their freshness and flavor. The combination of tomatoes with cucumber and red onion is a staple of this region, made in every home. It may seem simple—more an exercise in chopping than a recipe— but when the flavors of the herbs and vegetables come together, it is so worthwhile. It's the perfect accompaniment to almost anything, from breakfast falafels to a kofta supper. Ideally, prepare this salad an hour in advance to allow the flavors to marinate together before serving. It will only keep for a day or two in the fridge due to its fresh ingredients.

Makes: a side dish for 4–5

3 tablespoons olive oil
Juice of 2 limes
Salt and pepper
Handful of mint, stalks removed
    and finely chopped
Handful of parsley, stalks
    removed and finely chopped
1 medium red onion, diced
1 large cucumber
5 tomatoes, quartered

Time: 10 minutes

In a large salad bowl, mix the olive oil with the lime juice, salt and pepper to taste, and chopped herbs. Add the diced red onion and stir to combine.

Halve the cucumber lengthways, then again to quarter it, then chop into chunks. Add to the salad and stir.

Add the quartered tomatoes and stir them in. Place in the fridge for an hour before serving.

Quinoa Tabbouleh with Pickled Lime

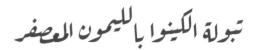

⊘ vegan   ⚕ protein-packed

Tabbouleh is a classic Syrian and Lebanese salad now eaten all over the world, thanks to its simplicity and the ready availability of its ingredients. Plus, it's delicious and so versatile—filling and heartwarming for all the family. In our version, the traditional tomato-cucumber-parsley-mint combo still forms the base, but protein-rich quinoa replaces bulgur wheat, and we add an extra kick with pickled lime and crunch with toasted seeds.

Makes: a side dish for 6–8

90 g (3 oz) quinoa (about ½ a cup)
Salt
1 kg (2 ¼ lb) cucumbers, deseeded and diced
2 large bunches parsley, stalks removed and finely chopped (about 2 cups)
Handful of mint, stalks removed and finely chopped
4 green onions, finely chopped
6 pickled limes, drained, rinsed, and diced
Handful of raisins (optional)
4 tablespoons sunflower seeds

For the dressing:
125 ml (½ cup) olive oil
Juice of 2 limes
Salt and pepper
2 tablespoons dried mint powder

Time: 40 minutes

Make the dressing first: put all of the ingredients into a glass jar, close the lid, and shake well to combine; alternatively, whisk them together in a small bowl.

Put the quinoa and 1 cup of hot water in a small pan over a medium heat, add salt, and bring to the boil. Lower the heat, cover, and let it simmer for 15 minutes, until cooked through. Fluff with a fork and set aside to cool.

In a dry skillet over a medium heat, toast the sunflower seeds for a couple of minutes.

To assemble the salad, put all the chopped vegetables and the quinoa in a large bowl, add half the dressing, and mix well. Follow with the herbs, raisins (if using), and pickled lime and mix again. Drizzle over the rest of the dressing and garnish with the toasted sunflower seeds.

Warm Lentil, Eggplant, and Pomegranate Salad

 vegan   protein-packed

This warm Levantine salad, known as *rummaniya* from the Arabic word for pomegranate, never ceases to delight our guests. Whenever we serve it among other mezze dishes, it's always one of the first to disappear. The combination of roasted eggplant with nutty lentils and the sweetness of pomegranate molasses is heavenly and so satisfying, full of protein and fiber. Anytime you're out of energy, or even just out of sorts, this dish makes such a comforting pick-you-up.

Makes: 4 servings

400 g (14 oz) brown lentils (about 2 cups)
1 teaspoon ground cumin
Salt and pepper
3 eggplants, cubed
4 tablespoons olive oil
3 garlic cloves, minced
4 tablespoons pomegranate molasses
Handful of pomegranate seeds
Handful of parsley, stalks removed and roughly chopped

Time: 40 minutes

Preheat the oven to 180°C (350°F/Gas mark 4).

Put the lentils, cumin, and 5 cups of water to cover in a medium pan. Bring to the boil, then lower the heat, cover, and let simmer for about 30 minutes or until the lentils are cooked through. Season with salt and pepper.

Arrange the eggplant cubes in one layer on an oven tray and brush with 2 tablespoons of the olive oil. Place in the middle of the oven for 20–25 minutes, turning halfway through.

Turn heat to low, and heat the remaining olive oil in a small skillet over a medium heat. Add the minced garlic and cook for a couple of minutes until golden (but not brown).

Add the hot fried garlic, roast eggplant, and pomegranate molasses to the pan of lentils and stir. Cook for another 5 minutes, then add the lime juice and remove from the heat.

Tip into a deep serving dish, and garnish with the pomegranate seeds, a drizzle of olive oil, and the chopped parsley. Serve warm.

Fattoush Salad

 vegan   paleo   🌾 gluten-free

The classic Middle Eastern salad, *fattoush* is made distinctive—and more substantial—by the addition of torn-up bread. Traditionally, it's a great way to use up yesterday's flatbreads, but we use gluten-free crackers here for a slightly lighter recipe. Sumac and mint are essential flavors for *fattoush* and we, like many others, love to add sweet-sour pomegranate molasses to the dressing. To combine the olive oil, syrupy molasses, and lime juice perfectly in no time, take our tip and shake the dressing ingredients together in a glass jar with a lid.

Makes: a side dish for 4

3 tomatoes, deseeded and cut into chunks
3 small cucumbers or 1 large cucumber, sliced
½ red bell pepper, deseeded and cut into squares
½ yellow bell pepper, deseeded and cut into squares
Handful of mint leaves
Handful of black (preferably Kalamata) olives, pitted (optional)
Gluten-free crackers, broken into 10–12 medium-sized squares

For the dressing:
1 garlic clove, minced
Juice of 3 limes
1 teaspoon pomegranate molasses
3 tablespoons extra-virgin olive oil
1 teaspoon sumac
Salt and pepper
1 red onion, thinly sliced

Time: 10 minutes

Add all of the dressing ingredients, except the onions, to a glass jar, seal the lid, and shake well. Add the sliced red onions.

Rinse the olives under running water to get rid of any excess brine, and pat dry with kitchen paper. Mix all the vegetables, the mint leaves, and the olives in a large bowl.

Give the dressing another shake and drizzle over the salad. Scatter over the broken crackers and serve.

Greek Fig Salad

 vegan  paleo

While this recipe is not purely Middle Eastern, all the cuisines of the countries surrounding the Mediterranean influence each other to a certain extent. We love to prepare this Greek-style salad for gatherings on the beach, because it is just so fresh and flavorful. While most of the ingredients are usually readily to hand, the addition of the goat's feta and sweet, ripe figs makes it look and taste special. Full of goodness and yumminess, this salad will definitely become a summer staple for your family and friends.

Makes: 4–5 servings

Handful walnuts, roughly
   chopped
3 small cucumbers or 1 large
   cucumber, roughly peeled and
   chopped
2 tomatoes, quartered
1 yellow bell pepper, deseeded
   and sliced
Handful of green olives, pitted
   and sliced
2 tablespoons thyme
Handful sliced cabbage
100 g (4 oz) goat's milk feta
   cheese, cut into cubes
5 fresh figs, quartered

For the dressing:
125 ml (½ cup) olive oil
3 tablespoons apple cider
   vinegar, or white vinegar
½ teaspoon raw honey
Juice of 2 limes
2 garlic cloves, minced
Salt and pepper
1 red onion, thinly sliced

Time: 20 minutes

Add all of the dressing ingredients to a small bowl, except the onion, and mix well (or shake together in a glass jar). Add the sliced red onion.

Toast the walnuts in a dry skillet over a medium heat for a couple of minutes. Set aside to cool.

In a medium bowl, mix together the sliced cucumber, tomatoes, pepper, onions, and olives. Sprinkle with half of the thyme, add the dressing, and toss to coat all of the vegetables.

Arrange the sliced cabbage at the bottom of a salad bowl or large serving dish. Tip the cucumber and tomato mix over it, spooning over all the dressing. Scatter over the toasted walnuts and feta cubes; place the fig quarters on top, and finish by sprinkling over the rest of the thyme.

Beet and Mint Salad

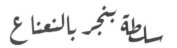

 vegan   paleo

This is a robust but refreshing salad with a gorgeous sweet-sour balance of flavors and contrasting textures. Rather than overpowering the sweet beets with vinegar, we team it instead with onions that have been lightly pickled, then add crunchy caramelized pecans, soft beans, peppery arugula and fresh green herbs, and a luscious but zesty dressing. Non-vegans could replace the coconut sugar with honey.

Makes: a side dish for 4–5

3 large beets
2 red onions, thinly sliced
125 ml (½ cup) white vinegar
60 g (2 oz) pecans, roughly chopped
1 tablespoon coconut sugar
2 cups arugula, or baby spinach
Handful of fresh mint leaves
Handful of parsley, stalks removed and roughly chopped
½ cup fresh broad (fava) beans, cooked

For the dressing:
1 garlic clove, minced
1 teaspoon dried mint
Juice of 2 limes
2 teaspoons pomegranate molasses
3 tablespoons extra-virgin olive oil
1 teaspoon sumac
Salt and pepper

Time: 60 minutes

Put the beets in a medium pan and fill with cold water. Bring to the boil then simmer over a medium-low heat for 30–40 minutes. Once the beets are cooked through, drain off the water and let them cool for a few minutes. Peel, and cut into cubes. Set aside to cool down completely.

While the beets cook, put the sliced red onions and vinegar in a bowl and let the onions steep for a few minutes. Drain and set aside.

In a dry skillet over a medium heat, toast the pecans for a minute, shaking the pan, then add the coconut sugar and stir until the sugar melts and caramelizes the pecans (about 3 minutes). Take the pan from the heat and place the caramelized pecans on a non-stick surface to cool.

Put all the ingredients for the dressing into a glass jar, secure the lid, and shake well to combine.

To assemble the salad, put the arugula, mint, and parsley in a large serving bowl and toss together. Drizzle over the dressing, toss again, then add the beets, onion, and beans. Sprinkle the pecans over the top, and serve.

Lentil, Beet, and Red Onion Salad

عدس بالبنجر والبصل الأحمر

⊘ vegan   ⚗ protein-packed

The big, earthy flavors of lentils and mineral-rich beets in this dish are partnered with a punchy dressing to make a hearty and heart-healthy salad. With warm gluten-free flatbread and a green salad it makes a complete and satisfying meal, although if you're non-vegan, you could crumble over some tangy goat's milk feta for a super-tasty boost.

Makes: 4 servings

3 medium beets
500 g (1 lb 2 oz) brown lentils
   (about 2 ½ cups)
1 teaspoon ground cumin
Salt and pepper
1 red onion, thinly sliced
60 ml (¼ cup) apple cider vinegar
   or white vinegar
60 ml (¼ cup) olive oil
Juice of 1 lime
Handful of parsley, stalks
   removed and chopped
1 tablespoon rosemary, stems
   removed and chopped
   (optional)

Time: 50 minutes

Put the beets in a medium pan and cover with cold water. Bring to the boil, then simmer over medium-low heat for 30–40 minutes, until cooked through.

While the beets cook, wash the lentils in a sieve under running water then place in a medium pot and cover with water. Add the cumin, and salt and pepper. Bring to the boil, then lower the heat and simmer for about 20 minutes, so that the lentils are cooked but not turning mushy.

Slice the onion and put in a small bowl with the vinegar to steep for 10 minutes.

When the lentils are done, drain and place in a salad bowl to cool. When the beets are cooked, drain and leave to cool for a few minutes, then peel, halve and slice them. Add them to the lentils, then drain the onions and pile on the top.

Drizzle over the olive oil and lime juice, garnish with the chopped parsley and rosemary, and serve.

Chickpea Belila

بليلة حمص

 vegan   protein-packed

People new to Middle Eastern cuisine are often surprised by just how plant-based and clean it is, full of nutritious, vegan dishes with lots of grains, greens, and herbs. Made tasty with spices and other flavorful ingredients, these chickpeas are just such a dish, and make a great, protein-filled pick-me-up or post-workout breakfast. Whether eaten warm or cold, nothing is more hearty yet light for the start or end of your day. Belila will keep in the fridge for up to a week, so we always make a big batch that the whole family can dip into and enjoy.

Makes: 4 servings

500 g (1 lb 2 oz) cooked
   chickpeas (about 2 ½ cups),
   (see Hummus on page 19 for
   cooking instructions)
2 tablespoons olive oil
4 green onions, chopped
4 garlic cloves, minced
2 teaspoons cumin
Salt and pepper
180 ml (¾ cup) vegetable stock
Handful fresh cilantro, stems
   removed and roughly chopped

Time: 20 minutes

In a large pan, heat the olive oil and sauté the green onions over a medium heat for a couple of minutes. Add the minced garlic and cook, stirring, for a couple more minutes, then tip in the cooked chickpeas. Add the cumin and season with salt and pepper, and mix to combine it all well.

Pour in the stock, bring to the boil then reduce the heat and let it simmer for about 5 minutes to bring all the flavors together.

Let it cool a bit before serving, garnished with cilantro.

Simple White Bean Salad

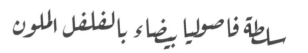

سلطة فاصوليا بيضاء بالفلفل الملون

⊘ vegan   ⊕ protein-packed

White beans are so common and familiar in Egypt that they don't even have a particular name. This versatile dish can be served hot as a snack or as a side, or cold as a salad or mezze. The beans are the perfect foil for flavorsome vegetables, all enlivened with a citrusy dressing and lots of fresh parsley. This dish will keep in the fridge for up to a week, and with time all the flavors blend.

You can use cannellini or navy beans in this recipe. We start with dried beans, soaking them in water overnight and then simmering for an hour on low heat before making the salad. You can substitute 2 400 g cans for this recipe, but drain and rinse the beans well under running water to remove the preservative liquid.

Makes: 2 large servings

1 tablespoon olive oil
2 stalks celery, finely chopped
2 green onions, finely chopped
1 small red bell pepper, diced
500 g (1 lb 2 oz) white beans
   (about 2 cups), cooked
Salt and pepper
Small bunch of parsley, stalks
   removed and finely chopped

For the dressing:
60 ml (¼ cup) extra-virgin olive
   oil
Juice of 2 limes
2 garlic cloves, minced
Salt and pepper

Time: 15 minutes

Heat the tablespoon of olive oil in a skillet, and sauté the celery, green onions, and pepper for a few minutes, until slightly softened. Set aside to cool.

Put the dressing ingredients in a small bowl and whisk to combine (or put them in a glass jar, close the lid securely, and shake well.)

When the beans are cool, tip them into a salad bowl and season with salt and pepper. Stir in the semi-cooked vegetables, then pour over the dressing. Finish with the freshly chopped parsley and toss the salad to make sure all is well combined.

Roasted Eggplant and Cauliflower Salad

ⓥ vegan   🍴 protein-packed

Sometimes you crave a crisp, leafy salad, but sometimes you want something more substantial. This flavorful salad is firmly in the latter camp, with the sweetness and warmth of roasted veggies beautifully complemented by the citrusy zing of sumac and orange. We sometimes use the Spicy Crispy Chickpeas recipe (see page 000) to make the crunchy garnish for this salad, but you can just roast plain cooked chickpeas with a small drizzle of olive oil for 30–40 minutes while the veggies are cooking. Toasted peeled hazelnuts also make a fine alternative.

Makes: a side dish for 4

2 medium eggplants, cut into 2.5 cm (1 in) cubes
Half a cauliflower, cut into florets (about 2 cups)
Salt and pepper
1 teaspoon sumac
About 3 tablespoons olive oil
A bunch of arugula leaves, stems removed (about 2 cups)
Handful of mint, stems removed
Handful of green olives, pitted and sliced
2 tablespoons roasted chickpeas or whole toasted hazelnuts
2 wedges fresh orange

Time: 40 minutes

Preheat the oven to 180°C (350°F/Gas mark 4). Line an oven tray with baking parchment, and brush the paper with olive oil.

Spread the eggplant cubes and cauliflower florets over the tray, and season with salt, pepper, and sumac. Drizzle over more olive oil and tumble the vegetables around to make sure all are well coated and seasoned. Place in the middle of the oven for about 30 minutes until cooked through, flipping the vegetables halfway through. Set aside to cool.

To assemble the salad, toss the arugula and mint in a shallow salad bowl. Season with salt and pepper and drizzle over a little more olive oil. Layer over the cooled eggplant and cauliflower, and sprinkle with the sliced olives and chickpeas. Squeeze the orange wedges and sprinkle a pinch of salt over the top, and serve.

Warm Freekeh and Eggplant Salad

 vegan

This is such a heartwarming and comforting salad, which can be served as a filling side dish or stand alone as a vegan meal, because nutritionally, it's the complete package. It's full of interest too, with each component adding a different texture and flavor to create a perfect balance. It's bound to win over any friends who have doubts about the "healthy lifestyle," and delight those that embrace it, too.

Makes: 6 large servings

3 tablespoons olive oil
1 onion, finely chopped
400 g (14 oz) freekeh, washed and drained (about 2 cups)
Salt and pepper
2 large eggplants, cut into 2.5 cm (1 in) cubes
1 red onion, thinly sliced
2 tablespoons white vinegar
½ cup pomegranate seeds
60 g (2 oz) pine nuts
Handful of purslane leaves or arugula
Handful of parsley, stalks removed and chopped

For the dressing:
4 tablespoons pomegranate molasses
2 tablespoons olive oil
Salt

Time: 40 minutes

Rinse the freekeh thoroughly in a sieve under cold running water.

In a medium pan, heat 2 tablespoons of the olive oil and sauté the chopped onion until soft (about 7 minutes). Add the freekeh, then pour in 4 cups of hot water and add salt and pepper.

Bring to the boil, then reduce the heat and leave to simmer, covered, until the freekeh is cooked and the water is absorbed (about 30 minutes).

While the freekeh cooks, preheat the oven to 180°C (350°F/Gas mark 4) and line an oven tray with baking parchment. Rub the eggplant cubes with the remaining olive oil, adding salt and pepper. Spread them out on the oven tray and place in the middle of the oven to roast for 25 minutes.

Put the onion slices and vinegar in a small bowl, and leave for 10 minutes. Drain the onions and squeeze out any excess moisture, then set aside.

In a dry skillet, toast the pine nuts for a couple of minutes, shaking the pan.

To assemble, in a large salad bowl, mix the cooked freekeh with the roasted eggplant, sliced red onions, pomegranate seeds, toasted pine nuts, purslane or arugula, and parsley. Drizzle over the pomegranate molasses and a little more olive oil, and add a sprinkling of salt. Serve warm or cold.

Freekeh, Lentil, and Chickpea Koshari

كشري الفريك بالعدس والحمص

⊘ vegan   ⚗ protein-packed

Koshari ranks up there with falafel among Egypt's most beloved recipes, one of the most popular street foods. We replaced the traditional white rice and macaroni with something more nutritious, while still retaining the dish's essential satisfying character.

The list of ingredients may look long, but each element is easy to prepare. Don't worry about coordinating your timing—all the components served hot can easily be kept warm until needed.

Makes: 6–8 servings

For the crispy onions:
1 kg (2 ¼ lb) onions, sliced
2 tablespoons oat flour, or any flour
3 tablespoons olive oil

For the vinegar garlic sauce:
5 garlic cloves, minced
1 tablespoon olive oil
125 ml (½ cup) vinegar

For the lentils:
300 g (10 ½ oz) brown lentils (1 ½ cups)
1 teaspoon ground cumin
Salt and pepper
1 tablespoon olive oil
90 g (3 oz) chickpeas, cooked (½ cup)
    (see Hummus on page 19 for cooking
    instructions)

For the freekeh:
2 tablespoons coconut or olive oil
1 onion, diced
400 g (14 oz) freekeh (2 cups)
1 cardamom pod
1 bay leaf
Salt and pepper

For the tomato sauce:
1 kg (2 ¼ lb) tomatoes, cut into chunks
1 tablespoon olive oil
6 garlic cloves, sliced
½ teaspoon chili powder (optional)
½ teaspoon cinnamon
Salt and pepper

Time: 60 minutes

For the onions, preheat the oven to 200°C (400°F/Gas Mark 6). Line a large oven tray with baking parchment, and brush it with olive oil. Pat the sliced onions dry with kitchen paper then dust them with the flour. Spread out the slices in one layer on the oven tray and drizzle over the olive oil. Toss the onions with your hands to coat with the oil. Bake for 30 minutes, tumbling them around every few minutes to make sure they cook evenly. When done, set aside.

For the vinegar garlic sauce, in a small pan, sauté the garlic in the olive oil for a couple of minutes, then add the vinegar and ¼ cup hot water. Bring to the boil, then lower the heat and simmer for 10 minutes. Set aside to cool.

To prepare the lentils, rinse them thoroughly in a sieve then place in a medium pan. Cover with about 2 cups of water and bring to the boil. Sprinkle in the cumin, salt and pepper, then lower the heat and simmer, covered, for 20–25 minutes until cooked through. Stir in the cooked chickpeas and olive oil for the last 5 minutes of cooking. Remove from the heat and drain over a bowl, reserving the liquid for the freekeh. Set the lentils aside, covered, to keep warm.

While the lentils are simmering, start cooking the freekeh, first rinsing it in a sieve under running water. Heat the coconut or olive oil in a medium pan and sauté the diced onion until golden (about 10 minutes). Stir in the freekeh and add the cardamom pod, bay leaf, and salt and pepper. Add up to 1 liter (4 cups) of water to the freekeh, cover, and simmer over a low heat for 30 minutes, or until cooked through. Remove the bay leaf and cardamom and fluff the freekeh with a fork, then add it to the cooked lentils and cover to keep warm.

Freekeh, Lentil, and Chickpea Koshari (cont.)

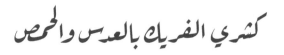

To prepare the tomato sauce, blend the tomatoes to a smooth consistency in a food processor or blender. In a medium pan, heat the olive oil and sauté the garlic until golden. Add the chili, if using, the tomato juice, cinnamon, and salt and pepper. Stir to combine, cover, and bring to a low simmer to thicken for about 20 minutes.

To assemble the *koshari*, use a deep serving dish. First, add the freekeh-lentil-chickpea mix, then drizzle over about half the tomato sauce and scatter over some of the crispy onions. Serve with the remaining tomato sauce, onions, and the garlic vinegar sauce in separate bowls, so that everyone can help themselves.

Quinoa-stuffed Caramelized Onions

محشي البصل بالكينوا

○ vegan   ⚖ protein-packed

These luscious onions with a traditional *mahshi* stuffing full of green herbs will be a healthy hit whether served as a main course or side dish. Quinoa absorbs the herbs and spice flavors so well here that your guests will not believe that it's not a rice stuffing. The onions are first caramelized to bring out some deep, sweet flavor, then cooked until meltingly tender in a tamarind broth.

Makes: 8 side servings

2 tablespoons coconut oil
20 small red onions
Salt and pepper
4 cups (1 liter) vegetable stock
3 tablespoons tamarind paste

For the stuffing:
2 tablespoons coconut oil
4 garlic cloves, minced
6 tomatoes, puréed
½ teaspoon cinnamon
Salt and pepper
350 g (12 ½ oz) quinoa, washed (about 2 cups)
3 tablespoons pomegranate molasses
Handful of mint, stems removed and finely chopped
Small bunch of parsley, stems removed and finely chopped
Small bunch of cilantro, stems removed and finely chopped
Handful of dill, finely chopped

Time: 50 minutes

In a skillet, heat coconut oil, and sauté the whole onions for about 10 minutes, or until lightly browned all over. Season with salt and pepper, and set aside to cool.

Cut a thin slice off the top of each onion then carefully hollow them out, leaving a strong shell. Dice all the onion you have removed.

To prepare the stuffing, heat 2 tablespoons coconut oil and sauté the diced onions for about 7 minutes, until translucent. Add the garlic and cook, stirring, for a couple more minutes.

Stir in the puréed tomato and cinnamon, add salt and pepper, and bring to the boil. Add the quinoa. Cover and cook for about 5 minutes, then drizzle over the pomegranate molasses and add all the chopped herbs. Give it a final stir before removing from the heat. The quinoa doesn't have to be cooked through.

Stuff each hollowed-out onion with one tablespoon of the stuffing mix. In a largish, deep pan, arrange all the onions at the base, sitting snugly together. Then repeat with two more layers.

Bring the vegetable stock to the boil and stir in the tamarind paste until dissolved. Pour over the stuffed onions and cook them, covered, on a medium heat for 30 minutes, until the onions and stuffing are cooked through and the liquid has thickened. You can add a little hot water during the cooking if needed to keep the onions moist. Serve warm.

Vine Leaf Pie

 فطيرة ورق عنب

 gluten-free   protein-packed

You want to impress your guests? Prepare a vine leaf pie. This is a light, fragrant and wholesome take on the Middle East's favorite stuffed vegetable dish *mahshi wara' 'enab*. It's a perfect main dish, and bringing the pie to the table, then cutting into it to release the lovely aromas of the filling, adds a touch of ceremony to any party or family gathering.

If you can't get hold of fresh vine leaves, you will find them bottled or frozen in any Middle Eastern grocery store, and even in some supermarkets.

Makes: 8 slices

20–25 vine leaves (fresh, frozen, or from a jar)
4 small onions, diced
4 tablespoons olive oil
1 tablespoon ghee
30 g (1 oz) pine nuts, and another tablespoon for garnish
400 g (14 oz) ground lamb meat
Handful of parsley, stems removed and finely chopped
Handful of dill, finely chopped
Bunch of mint, stems removed and finely chopped (about ½ cup)
Zest and juice of 1 lime
90 g (3 oz) cooked quinoa (about ½ cup)
3 tablespoons flax seeds, preferably ground
Salt and pepper

Time: 50 minutes

Preheat the oven to 190°C (375°F/Gas mark 5).

If using fresh or frozen (defrost first) vine leaves, put them in a shallow bowl, pour boiling water over them and leave for 10 minutes, then dry on a clean dish towel. Trim off and discard the tough stem at the base of each leaf. Bottled leaves do not need blanching or trimming, just wash them under running water to remove the brine. Set aside.

Sauté the diced onions in 1 tablespoon of the olive oil until golden brown. Set aside to cool.

In a dry skillet over a medium heat, toast the pine nuts for a few minutes, shaking the pan. Set aside.

In a small bowl, mix the ghee with 2 tablespoons of the olive oil and set aside.

To prepare the stuffing, in a medium bowl, mix the onions, pine nuts (leaving some aside for garnish), ground lamb, herbs, and cooked quinoa. Season with salt and pepper.

To prepare the pie, brush a 20 cm (8 in) round baking pan or dish generously with the ghee-olive oil mix. Line the base and sides with vine leaves (rough side up), letting them drape over the sides.

Spread the stuffing mix evenly over the vine leaves and press it down to form a firm, even layer. Fold the overhanging leaves over the top, then use more leaves to cover the whole of the top. Brush with the remaining ghee mix, and sprinkle the ground flax seeds all over the top.

Bake in the preheated oven for 40 minutes, or until the top crisps and the flax seeds turn golden brown. Remove from the oven, sprinkle with toasted pine nuts and leave to cool for 10 minutes before slicing. Serve warm.

Black-eyed Pea and Spinach Stew

 vegan    protein-packed

This is a heartwarming stew, super-filling and delicious. You can serve it with quinoa, or by itself as a nourishing "superfood bowl." Kids love this dish: the beans are easy to eat (when well-cooked, they melt in your mouth), the tomatoes add sweetness, and the spinach isn't overpowering. Nutty black-eyed peas are full of fiber, potassium, and protein, very low in fat, with what's called resistant starch – the kind that "resists" digestion-making them the ultimate legume for weight-watchers and clean-eaters.

Makes: 4 servings

2 tablespoons olive oil
1 large onion, diced
2 garlic cloves, sliced
3 tomatoes, diced, with their juices
1 teaspoon ground cumin
Salt and pepper
500 g (1 lb 2 oz) black-eyed peas
500 ml (2 cups) hot vegetable stock
Handful of baby spinach leaves

Time: 30 minutes + overnight soaking time

Rinse the peas in a sieve under running water, place in a bowl, fill with cold water and leave overnight to soak.

When you're ready to cook, add the olive oil to a large pan over a medium heat, and gently sauté the onions and garlic until translucent.

Add the tomatoes, the cumin, and salt and pepper. Stir for a couple of minutes, then add the peas, followed by the hot stock. Bring to the boil then lower the heat, cover, and let simmer for 15 minutes. You want about half the liquid to reduce before adding the spinach.

When the peas are tender, add the spinach leaves and stir them in. As soon as they have wilted, remove from the heat and serve hot.

Veggies & Greens

خضار وخضرة

Roasted Winter Vegetables with Sumac Vinaigrette

 vegan   protein-packed

Full of roasted winter veggies combined in a flavor fiesta, this recipe is filling, good for you, and most importantly super-delicious. The ingredients aren't written in stone: you can use almost anything in the fridge, in any sort of quantity—this may be a crowd-pleasing side dish, but cold leftovers make a super lunchtime salad bowl too. Roasting brings out a sweetness in vegetables that is perfectly complemented by our tangy vinaigrette dressing.

Sumac, if you're unfamiliar with it, is a citrusy, deep red spice popular in the Levantine area of the Middle East; it's used in salad dressings, most notably for fattoush, and is often added to marinades for chicken. Keep a jar in your pantry to add instant oomph to your dishes!

Makes: a side dish for 6

3 fennel bulbs, quartered
4 carrots, cut into wedges
2 red onions, quartered
Half a cauliflower, cut into florets (about 2 cups)
170 g (6 oz) Brussels sprouts
3 tablespoons olive oil
50 g (about 2 oz) cooked chickpeas (optional) (see Hummus on page 19 for cooking instructions)

For the dressing:
60 ml (¼ cup) olive oil
2 tablespoons white or apple cider vinegar
2 teaspoons Dijon mustard
1 teaspoon sumac
1 garlic clove, minced
Salt and pepper

Time: 45 minutes

Preheat the oven to 180°C (350°F/Gas mark 4). Line an oven tray or pan with baking parchment.

Spread out all the veggies on the tray and drizzle with olive oil. Place in the middle of the oven for 30–40 minutes, until all are cooked through. After 20 minutes in the oven, tumble the veggies around a bit and add the chickpeas (if using them), then return to the oven for the remaining time.

While the vegetables roast, prepare the dressing by whisking all the ingredients together in a bowl (or shaking in a glass jar) and set aside.

When the veggies are done, tip them onto a serving platter, drizzle over the dressing, and serve warm.

Green Beans with Caramelized Onions

 vegan   gluten-free   paleo

If you're on the strictest paleo diet, then green beans are technically classed as a legume, and so are off-limits. Look away, then, while we introduce this addictively tasty recipe for these simple veggies, packed with green goodness, low in calories, and free from saturated fat. The combination of garlicky green beans with sugar-free caramelized onion and walnuts is so delicious, yet so easy to prepare; it never fails to impress as a versatile side dish. We've served it with a favorite party piece, the Whole Baked Fish with Tahini (see page 171), and it totally hit the spot for us and our guests.

Makes: 2–3 servings

500 g (1 lb 2 oz) green beans, trimmed
115 g (4 oz) walnuts, roughly chopped (about 1 cup)
3 tablespoons olive oil
8 garlic cloves, thinly sliced
5 onions, thinly sliced
Salt and pepper
2 teaspoons finely chopped fresh thyme leaves

Time: 40 minutes

Blanch the beans in a large pan of salted boiling water until bright green in color (about 2 minutes). Drain the beans and immediately plunge them into a bowl of cold or iced water to stop the cooking process and keep them crisp. Lift them out and set aside.

In a large dry skillet on medium heat, toast the chopped walnuts for a few minutes, and set aside.

In the same pan, heat 1 tablespoon of the olive oil and sauté the garlic for a couple of minutes, until browned. Lift the garlic out and set aside.

Return the pan to the heat and add the rest of the olive oil. Add the onions and season with salt and pepper. Cook, stirring frequently, until the onions caramelize (about 20–25 minutes). Add the thyme, and cook for another 5 minutes. Add the green beans, walnuts, and garlic, and stir well to combine, then remove from the heat. Adjust the seasoning, if necessary, and serve warm.

Street-style Crispy Baked Cauliflower and Broccoli

 gluten-free

Fried cauliflower florets are often cooked up by falafel street vendors in this region as part of a lavish breakfast meal, adding their delicious crispiness to fried eggplant, soft beans, tahini, and pickles. Here's a recreated homemade recipe celebrating their amazing tastiness and nutritional values without the "fried junk" guilt. We partner the cauliflower with broccoli, a newer crop to the Middle East but one that's a perfect match.

Makes: a side dish for 4

60 ml (¼ cup) olive oil
1 medium cauliflower head (about 300 g /10 ½ oz)
2 medium broccoli heads (about 300 g /10 ½ oz)
3 eggs
2 tablespoons ground cumin
1 tablespoon ground coriander
1 teaspoon chili powder
1 tablespoon salt
1 teaspoon black pepper
90 g (3 oz) oat flour (about 1 cup)

Time: 40 minutes

Preheat the oven to 200°C (400°F/Gas Mark 6) and line an oven tray with baking parchment, then brush the paper with 1 tablespoon of the olive oil.

Cut the cauliflower and broccoli into medium-sized florets (with the small stems) and put them in a medium pan. Cover with hot water, bring to the boil, and cook uncovered for 8 minutes. Drain well and set aside.

In a bowl, mix the eggs with the rest of the olive oil, cumin, chili powder, and salt and pepper.

Carefully roll each floret in the oat flour, then in the egg mix, making sure they are all well covered.

Lay the florets out on the oven tray and place in the oven for 10 minutes, then turn them over to color on the other side and cook for another 10 minutes. If they're stubborn about turning golden, pop them under the broiler for 2 minutes. Whatever the case, serve hot!

Lime and Herb Artichokes

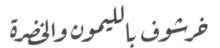

 vegan   gluten-free   paleo

Ranking among the top antioxidant foods, artichokes are delicious when coupled with citrus and herbs. They're an important crop in Egypt, and we love to eat them fresh, but we have to admit that frozen artichoke hearts, which are already semicooked, make this dish so quick and easy to prepare that it's one of our go-to recipes after a busy day.

Makes: a side dish for 4

750 g (1 ½ lbs) artichoke hearts, from frozen
3 tablespoons olive oil
5 garlic cloves, minced
Zest and juice of 4 limes
125 ml (½ cup) vegetable stock
Handful of parsley, finely chopped
Handful of dill, finely chopped
Salt and pepper

Time: 30 minutes

Rinse the artichoke hearts and cut them into halves.

In a sauté pan, heat the olive oil over medium heat. Sauté the garlic with half of the lime zest for a couple of minutes. Add the halved artichokes, and season with salt and pepper. Stir until the artichokes take on a golden color (about 10 minutes).

Add all the lime juice and the stock. Lower the heat, cover, and let simmer, stirring occasionally, until the artichokes are tender (about 15 minutes).

A minute before you take the pan off the heat, sprinkle over the parsley and dill, stir once more, and serve warm. Scatter over the rest of the lime zest for extra zing.

Carrot, Sweet Potato, and Herb Fritters

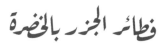

 gluten-free

Crispy, sweet, and herby, these veggie-packed fritters are to die for. They make a super side dish but are also such a nutrition-packed favorite for our kids' supper, or even cold in a lunchbox. While they're traditionally deep-fried, we bake the fritters in the oven, brushed with olive oil. We think they taste even better this way, and they're certainly lighter on the stomach.

Makes: 12–14 Pieces

3 tablespoons olive oil
3 eggs
2 teaspoons ground cumin
1 teaspoon ground coriander
Zest of 1 lime
Salt and pepper
4 carrots, grated
1 large sweet potato, grated
3 green onions, finely chopped
Small bunch of parsley, finely
   chopped (about ½ cup)
Handful of dill, finely chopped
   (about ¼ cup)

Time: 40 minutes

Preheat the oven to 180°C (350°F/Gas mark 4). Line an oven tray with baking parchment and brush with a little olive oil.

In a large bowl, whisk the eggs with the cumin, coriander, lime zest, and salt and pepper.

Place the grated carrot and sweet potato on a clean dish towel, roll it up to make a fat cylinder shape, grasp an end in each hand and twist in opposite directions for a few seconds to squeeze out excess liquid.

Add the carrot and sweet potato to the eggs along with the green onions, parsley, and dill.

Mix it through then use your hands to form fat patty shapes, using 2 to 3 tablespoons of mix per fritter. Place them on the oven tray then brush each with a little olive oil.

Bake in the middle of the oven for 20 minutes, turning them halfway through. Wait for a few minutes for them to cool a bit, before moving them from the hot tray.

Vegan Moussaka

 vegan paleo   gluten-free

If there is any dish that screams Middle East it is moussaka. The version that has traveled widely around the world is the Greek dish, which uses a béchamel sauce, but this recipe, with succulent eggplant, a thick, sweet and spicy tomato sauce, lashings of olive oil, and pops of warm sweetness from raisins, is the real deal. Traditionally, Middle Easterners cook the tomato sauce with ground meat, but we prefer this vegan version because it's lighter and celebrates the flavors of tomato and eggplant more; we cut the eggplants thickly for meatier chunks.

Makes: 6 generous servings

4 tablespoons olive oil
4 medium eggplants, thickly sliced
2 tomatoes, sliced
2 tablespoons raisins

For the tomato sauce:
6 tomatoes, peeled and cut into chunks
2 tablespoons olive oil
4 garlic cloves, minced
2 tablespoons thyme
½ teaspoon ground cinnamon
Salt and pepper

Time: 60 minutes

Preheat the oven to 180°C (350°F/Gas mark 4). Line a large oven tray with baking parchment, and brush with olive oil.

Arrange the eggplant slices side by side on the tray and brush them generously with olive oil. Place in the middle of the oven for about 30 minutes, turning them halfway through.

Brush the tomato slices with olive oil on both sides, place them on another tray, and add to the oven to roast for 15 minutes.

While the vegetables roast, prepare the tomato sauce. Put the fresh tomatoes into a food processor and blend, adding a drizzle of water if it'll help get them smooth.

In a saucepan, sauté the garlic in olive oil for a couple of minutes. Add the puréed tomatoes and bring to a boil. Add ½ cup hot water, stir, and lower the heat. Simmer uncovered for 20 minutes, then add the cinnamon and thyme, and season with salt and pepper. Cook, stirring, for another minute and take it off the heat.

To assemble the moussaka, start by brushing a 30 by 20 cm (12 by 8 in) oven dish with some of the tomato sauce. Arrange a layer of eggplant slices, filling gaps with tomato slices. Add one large ladleful of the tomato sauce and spread it evenly over the eggplant, then scatter over half the raisins. Add another layer of eggplant, tomato, tomato sauce, and the rest of the raisins. Add a final layer of eggplant and any remaining tomato, brush just a little tomato sauce on top, and bake for 20 minutes. Serve hot, with warm flatbreads.

Chili Okra "Weika"

بامية ويكا

Okra is a popular crop in the Middle East, often cooked in onion and tomato sauce and eaten with white rice. In Upper Egypt, which is where most of Egypt's okra is grown, we don't use tomatoes, but instead load it with chili and herbs, and that's the recipe we share here. It's eaten with crusty bread, dipping it into the creamy okra bowl then sucking in all the yummy garlicky, coriander, and chili flavors. When the okra's cooked through, some people whizz it in a food processor for an even creamier, soupy texture, but we prefer to leave it with some texture, preparing the *tasha* (garlic coriander mix), while it's still on the stove.

This recipe can easily be made vegan by replacing the bone broth with vegetable stock, or just salted water with a cardamom pod and bay leaf popped in.

Pickled limes make a great accompaniment to this dish.

Makes: 6 servings

500 g (1 lb 2 oz) small okra
750 ml (3 cups) bone broth (see Bone Broth on page 59)
½ red chili pepper, thinly sliced
Salt and pepper
2 tablespoons coconut oil
3 garlic cloves, minced
1 teaspoon chili powder (optional)
2 teaspoons ground coriander
Handful of cilantro, finely chopped

Time: 45 minutes

Wash the okra, remove the stems, and slice it into small rings. Place it in a heavy-bottomed pan along with the broth and sliced chili. Bring to the boil on high heat, then reduce the heat and cover. Let it simmer for about 30 minutes; just before the end, season with salt and pepper.

At this point, if you want a smooth consistency, pulse the okra in a food processor; otherwise leave on the stove to keep warm.

In a small pan, heat up the coconut oil and sauté the minced garlic, ground coriander, and (if using) chili powder for a minute, then tip them over the okra. Add the chopped cilantro and give everything a final stir before taking it off the stove.

Green Beans with Carrots and Tomatoes

فاصوليا بالجزر والطماطم

⊘ vegan   ⊗ paleo   ⊛ gluten-free

Green beans are eaten a lot in most Middle Eastern countries. In Lebanon, they're cooked in olive oil with chili and tomato, while in Egypt, the beans usually have a minced onion and tomato sauce. This recipe is close to the latter dish, but adds some extra fresh tomato and carrot. The carrot brings out the sweetness in the green beans and thickens the sauce, making the dish more filling and tasty. Serve it with brown rice or some crusty bread to mop up the sauce.

Makes: a side dish for 4

2 tablespoons olive oil
1 large onion, sliced
1 large carrot, grated
500 g (1 lb 2 oz) green beans, trimmed and cut into 3 cm (1 in) lengths
4 tomatoes, puréed
Pinch of cinnamon
2 bay leaves
450 ml (2 cups) vegetable stock or water
3 tomatoes, diced
Salt and pepper

Time: 45 minutes

Heat the olive oil in a medium heavy-bottomed pan and sauté the onion gently, until translucent (about 7 minutes). Add the grated carrot and cook for another 3 minutes, stirring occasionally.

Add the green beans, season with salt and pepper, and stir. Add the puréed tomatoes, cinnamon, and bay leaves. When the juice starts bubbling, add the hot broth or water. Bring back to a boil, then cover and lower the heat to a simmer.

After about 20 minutes, stir in the diced tomatoes and adjust the seasoning if needed. Bring back to a simmer and cook, covered, for another 5–10 minutes until the beans are soft and the sauce has thickened a little. Remove bay leaves and serve hot.

Khobeiza

خوبيزة

(icon) protein-packed

Khobeiza is a member of the mallow family whose leaves are used in Egyptian cooking, as is the closely related *molokhiya* (see page 145). Like all dark green leafy veggies, it's powerfully healthy, rich in antioxidants, but what's distinctive is its texture, which is slippery, very much like okra (another plant relative).

The important thing when preparing *khobeiza* is to trim all the tough stalks and any thick midribs from the leaves, so that when chopped and cooked they wilt to become tender, nutritious green mouthfuls, stuffed with goodness.

If you don't have access to *khobeiza*, spinach would be a fair substitute. Vegans can use vegetable stock instead of the chicken stock, making sure they are generous with the salt.

Makes: 6 servings

1 kg (2 ¼ lb) *khobeiza*
Handful of chard (with stems)
Small bunch of dill
Small bunch of cilantro
1 liter (4-5 cups) chicken broth
½ cup freekeh (optional)
Salt and pepper
2 tablespoons olive oil
8 garlic cloves, minced
3 tablespoons ground coriander
Juice of 1 lime

Time: 30 minutes

Remove all stems and tough leaves from the *khobeiza* and put it, with all the green herbs, in a food processor. To make sure everything chops finely, don't overstuff it; do it in two batches if necessary.

In a large pan over a medium heat, bring the chicken broth to the boil. If using freekeh, wash under running water and add to the stock. Let it simmer for 5-10 minutes.

Remove any hard stems or thick leaves that have resisted the food processor before adding the chopped greens to the pot. Season generously with salt and pepper and let it simmer, covered, for 15 minutes.

While the greens cook, heat the olive oil in a small pan. Add the garlic and ground coriander and cook for a couple of minutes. Straight from the pan, tip the hot garlic mixture into the *khobeiza* as it is still cooking; you should hear a satisfying 'tshhhh' as the hot components coincide.

Give everything a final stir, drizzle lime juice over the top, and serve hot.

Lime Cauliflower Rice

 vegan    paleo

Cauliflower "rice" makes a fantastic substitute for gluten-full rice and pasta. Its high fiber content makes it filling, it's just as quick to prepare, and in addition to that, cauliflower is a superfood, packed with anti-inflammatory properties and cancer-fighting antioxidants. Cauliflower may be a little bland, but it readily absorbs other flavors, which is why it makes such a good side dish, soaking up all the juices from, say, chicken or fish. You can equally well add flavor before serving it, and this garlic and lime combination, along with the freshness of the chopped parsley, makes it just so delicious that you could eat it by itself.

Makes: a side dish for 4

1 medium cauliflower head
2 tablespoons olive oil
2 garlic cloves, minced
Pinch of chili powder (optional)
Salt and pepper
Small bunch parsley, stems
   removed and finely chopped
   (about ½ cup)
Zest of 2 limes
Juice of 1 lime
2 tablespoons toasted sliced
   almonds or pine nuts (optional)

Time: 20 minutes

Cut the cauliflower into medium-sized chunks, discarding the core. Working in batches, pulse the chunks in a food processor until they are broken into tiny pieces, maybe just a bit bigger than couscous. Wrap the cauliflower rice in a clean dish towel, and twist to squeeze out as much water as possible.

To a large skillet over a medium heat, add the olive oil and sauté the garlic for about 30 seconds, then add the cauliflower, chili, and salt and pepper, and stir to combine.

Cook, stirring occasionally, until the cauliflower turns slightly golden (about 8 minutes).

Remove from the heat, then stir in the chopped parsley and lime zest and juice. Adjust the seasoning if necessary and garnish, if desired, with toasted almonds or pine nuts.

Walnut Cabbage Rolls

⊘ vegan   🏋 protein-packed

We're guessing this recipe drifted down to us from Turkey, where walnuts are such a major crop. Rice is usually used for the stuffing, but we've swapped it out for protein-rich quinoa and this, together with the nuts and veggies, makes these little packages punch well above their weight nutrition-wise. Wonderfully moist and tender, they make a perfect supper dish.

Makes: around 16 rolls

1 white cabbage
1 tablespoon olive oil
1 onion, diced
1 carrot, diced
½ red bell pepper, diced
½ teaspoon paprika
Salt and pepper
60 g (2 oz) walnuts, roughly chopped (about ½ cup)
170 g (6 oz) quinoa, cooked (about 1 cup)
Handful of dill, finely chopped
Handful of parsley, finely chopped (plus extra for garnishing)
2 tomatoes, puréed
1 small tomato, sliced
Handful parsley, stems removed and roughly chopped

Time: 45 minutes

Heat a large pot of water to the boil. Season with salt.

Separate whole leaves from the cabbage; set aside a couple of large ones, and put the rest into the boiling water. Cover and cook for a few minutes, until tender. Drain well.

With a sharp knife, make a V-shaped cut to remove the lower half of the thick midrib of each cooked leaf, for easier rolling. Set them aside.

Heat the olive oil in a sauté pan, add the onion, and cook for about 5 minutes, until softened. Add the carrot and pepper and sauté for a few minutes more, then stir in the paprika and season with salt and pepper. Remove from the heat, and stir in the cooked quinoa, walnuts, dill, and parsley.

Roughly chop the raw set-aside cabbage leaves, then place half in the bottom of a medium pot to protect your cabbage rolls from the heat.

To make the rolls, lay a leaf flat and draw the V-shaped cut sides together, if possible to overlap a little. Place 1 tablespoon of mixture on one end; roll once, then fold in the sides, then continue rolling to completely enclose the filling. Repeat until you have no more filling. Set the rolls in layers in the pot on top of a bottom layer of chopped cabbage, and put the rest of the chopped cabbage on top.

Mix the puréed tomatoes with about 1 cup hot water and pour over the cabbage, then lay the slices of tomato on top. Cover and bring to the boil over a low to medium heat, reduce the heat and simmer for about 20 minutes. Transfer to a serving dish, sprinkle with chopped parsley, and serve warm.

Spinach Chips

 رقائق السبانخ

 vegan   paleo   gluten-free

A crispy, tasty, and highly nutritious, guilt-free snack—could anyone ask for more? The only tricky part of this tick-all-the-right-boxes treat is getting the baking time just right so you get crispy (not soggy and not burned) spinach! Ovens vary, as do spinach leaves, and the amount of oil needs careful judging too: if you add too much oil they'll take forever in the oven.

These are the measurements that work for us, but use them as guidelines only and season as you like to achieve your perfect chips. Two things to remember: one, spinach shrinks in the oven, just as when you cook it on the stove, so a big bag of raw spinach reduces to a bowl of chips; and, two, the key to success is for the spinach leaves to be completely dry, so wash them in the morning to make chips in the evening.

Makes: 2 servings

1 kg (2 ¼ lb) spinach, stems removed
2 tablespoons coconut oil
Salt and pepper
1 teaspoon paprika
Chili powder, to taste

Time: 15 minutes + drying time

Six hours or so before cooking, trim the stems from the spinach and wash it, then lay out on clean dish towels to dry completely.

Preheat the oven to 200°C (400°F/Gas Mark 6) and line a large oven tray with baking parchment. Brush the paper with coconut oil, dabbing some on the underside to make sure it sticks to the tray.

Spread the leaves out on the tray in one layer to allow them all to cook (you may need to cook them in batches). Drizzle over the remaining coconut oil, and sprinkle over the paprika, chili powder, and salt and pepper.

Place in the oven for 8–10 minutes. You need to keep an eye on it near the end to make sure the spinach doesn't darken too much. Remove from the oven and let rest for a minute or two, then eat immediately!

Roasts &
Grills

اللحوم

Baked Chicken with Sweet Potato

 protein-packed   🌾 gluten-free

Sanniyat firakh, literally 'tray of chicken,' must be the most popular home-cooked dish in Middle Eastern cuisine. Every family passes down its own recipe for perfectly moist and succulent, tasty birds. It's often cooked with sliced potatoes and onions added to the baking tray and served with rice to make a really substantial meal.

In this recipe, we try to maximize the nutritional benefits of this dish, and add some sweetness to its flavor profile with sweet potatoes and a sprinkle of cinnamon in the tomato juice. The result is a hearty, comforting dish that will become a regular family favorite on your table.

Makes: 3-4 servings

2 tablespoons olive oil
4 tomatoes, peeled
1 onion, very finely chopped
3 garlic cloves, minced
2 teaspoons ground cinnamon
1 teaspoon paprika
Salt and pepper
1 chicken, quartered
2 tablespoons finely chopped
   oregano
2 sweet potatoes, peeled and cut
   into cubes

Time: 60 minutes + marinating time

Put the peeled tomatoes into a food processor and pulse to a thick juice.

In a large pan, heat the olive oil and sauté the onion and garlic for a couple of minutes. Add the tomato juice and bring to a light boil, and sprinkle in half of the cinnamon and half of the paprika. Season with salt and pepper to taste, then remove from the heat and let it cool for a few minutes.

In the meantime, place the chicken quarters in a mixing bowl. Tip the cooled tomato mix over the chicken and make sure each piece is completely coated. Sprinkle over 1 tablespoon of the chopped oregano and cover the bowl with plastic wrap. Place in the fridge for 1 hour to marinate.

To cook the chicken, preheat the oven to 180°C (350°F/Gas mark 4). Spread out the chicken pieces in an oven tray or baking dish and bake in the middle of the oven for 30 minutes.

While the chicken bakes, peel and cube the sweet potatoes and parboil, for about 10 minutes, you don't want them cooked through yet. Remove from the heat and drain, then season with the remaining cinnamon, paprika, and oregano, and more salt and pepper if desired.

Add the sweet potatoes to the tray of chicken and return to the oven for another 15 minutes, or until the chicken is completely cooked through. Serve hot, straight from the oven.

Chicken Messakhan

 paleo   protein-packed

We make this often, not just because it's simple and delicious, but also because of the heavenly smells that fill the kitchen as it cooks. First there's the deep aroma of the onions as they slowly caramelize, then all the savoriness of the baking chicken, fragrant with herbs and spices, and finally the toasty pine nuts and the lovely green freshness of parsley. Have some crusty bread or freekeh ready to indulge in the olive oil–onion–sumac sauce that will be left in the pan after baking.

Makes: 6–8 servings

2 whole chickens, quartered
6 onions, sliced
4 red onions, sliced
4 garlic cloves, minced
3 tablespoons sumac
1 tablespoon salt
Generous grinding of black
   pepper
Handful of pine nuts, to garnish
Handful of parsley, stalks
   removed and chopped

For the marinade:
60 ml (¼ cup) olive oil
2 tablespoons sumac
Salt and pepper
2 tablespoons fresh thyme leaves
4 garlic cloves, minced
Handful of parsley, with stalks
   chopped.

Time: 75 minutes + marinating time

In a small bowl, mix all the marinade ingredients together. Arrange the chicken snugly in an oven tray or dish. Spoon over the marinade and use your hands to massage it into the chicken. Cover with cling film and place in the fridge for a couple of hours to marinate.

In the meantime, heat the olive oil in a large pan; add all the onions and stir in the sumac, salt and pepper. Turn the heat down low and sauté the onions slowly and gently for about 25 minutes until golden-brown, stirring occasionally to prevent them from sticking.

When you're ready to cook, preheat the oven to 180°C (350°F/Gas mark 4).

Uncover the chicken and spoon over the cooked onions. Drizzle over about ½ cup hot water to ensure the chicken stays moist, then bake uncovered in the middle of the oven for about 45 minutes, or until the chicken is completely cooked through.

Just before serving, toast the pine nuts for a couple of minutes in a dry skillet over a medium heat. Sprinkle over the chicken along with the fresh chopped parsley.

Moroccan Chicken Fillets with Green Olive and Harissa Salsa

صدور الفراخ بالهريسة والزيتون الأخضر

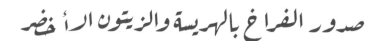

 paleo   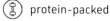 protein-packed

Almonds and olives often feature together in Moroccan cuisine, most especially in chicken tagines, and we've adapted that combination to create a lighter, fresher, faster dish that you can prepare much of in advance. The salsa can rest in the fridge for hours, or even overnight, until you're ready to cook the chicken. Tasty and filling, it needs only the simplest accompaniments, such as sautéed zucchini or carrots. You can use chopped dried apricots instead of the raisins.

Harissa is a wonderful, fiery Moroccan spice paste that is now readily found in supermarkets. If you're cautious about heat, start small, then gradually increase once you get a taste for it.

Makes: 3-4 servings

750 g (1½ lb) chicken breast fillets (or skinless chicken breasts sliced thinly cross-wise)

For the marinade:
1 teaspoon ground cardamom
½ teaspoon cinnamon
2 teaspoons ground coriander
Juice of 1 lime
2 teaspoons olive oil

For the salsa:
2 tomatoes, diced
Salt
2 tablespoons olive oil
2 teaspoons harissa paste (or more to your liking)
3 tablespoons raisins
Handful of almonds
Handful of green olives, pitted and chopped
Black pepper
Handful of cilantro, stems removed and finely chopped

Time: 45 minutes + 1 hour to marinate

Pat the chicken fillets dry with kitchen paper. Put them in a bowl and sprinkle over the cardamom, cinnamon, and coriander, turning the fillets to coat with spices on all sides. Drizzle over the lime juice and a little of the olive oil, then cover with plastic wrap and place in the fridge to marinate for an hour or so.

In the meantime, prepare the salsa. Dice the tomatoes, put them in a medium bowl and season with salt to allow them to release their juices. Stir in the rest of the olive oil and the harissa, and set aside.

In a separate bowl, soak the raisins in lukewarm water for 10 minutes.

Toast the almonds for a couple of minutes in a dry skillet over medium heat. Then chop them coarsely and add to the tomato mix, followed by the olives and a good grinding of black pepper. Drain the raisins and add them to the mix. Stir all to combine and set aside until you cook the chicken.

When you're ready to cook, set a large grill or sauté pan on a medium heat, then grill the chicken fillets for 8-10 minutes on each side, depending on their thickness (no need to add oil to pan since the marinade has enough). Lay them in a serving dish, stir the chopped cilantro into your salsa, and spoon it over the chicken.

Chicken Breast with Walnut Sauce (Sharkasiya)

شركسية

 protein-packed   gluten-free

This walnut sauce dish came to Egypt with the Turks, and it's become a popular treat for large gatherings like the Ramadan evening meal, or indeed any celebration. Traditionally, it's made with ordinary white bread, but we've found that the sauce is just as creamy a delight if you substitute gluten-free. Walnuts are a great source of omega-3 fatty acids and protein, so if you don't eat meat, make this easy sauce with a vegetable stock and eat it simply over quinoa or cauliflower rice for a filling, nutritious bowlful that will still taste amazing. Once prepared, the sauce will keep in the fridge for a couple of days or in the freezer for up to a month.

Makes: 3–4 servings

4 whole skinless, boneless chicken breasts
1 small onion, thinly sliced
1 stick of celery, sliced
Handful of cilantro, with stems
2 garlic cloves, minced
2 bay leaves
2 cardamom pods
½ teaspoon salt
1 teaspoon peppercorns
1 liter (4 cups) water

For the walnut sauce:
4 slices gluten-free bread, toasted
225 g (8 oz) walnuts (about 2 cups)
Generous pinch of nutmeg
1 teaspoon paprika
Salt and pepper

Time: 45 minutes

Put the chicken breasts in a pan big enough for them to sit side by side, and cover with all the vegetables, herbs, and seasonings. Pour in enough water to cover.

Bring to the boil over a medium to high heat. You'll see some white foam collecting on the surface as the water comes to a boil; skim this off, and reduce the heat to a simmer. Cover, and let the chicken cook for 15 minutes.

Transfer the chicken breasts to a serving plate. Their cooking liquid—basically, a quick chicken stock—will form the base for the sauce, so strain it into a bowl, discarding the rest of the ingredients.

Soak the toasted bread (it can be toasted by placing in an oven or toaster oven for 5–7 minutes at 180°C, 350°F/Gas mark 4) for a few seconds in the stock to soften slightly.

In a food processor, blend the walnuts into a smooth paste, then add the soaked bread and blend again. Gradually, add 500 ml (2 cups) of the stock while blending, until the mixture is smooth and creamy. Add the nutmeg, paprika, and salt and pepper to taste.

Spoon the walnut sauce into a pan over a medium heat, and let it warm and thicken for 10 minutes or so. If it seems too thick, add some more cooking liquid. Pour it hot over the chicken to serve.

Molokhiya Bourani-style

ملوخية بوراني

paleo   protein-packed

Molokhiya bourani is a lavish dish commonly prepared around Ramadan in Lebanon and Palestine. In Egypt, *molokhiya*—the leaves of a mallow plant, very like *khobeiza* (see page 127)—is usually served as a green soup, minced very finely and cooked in lots of stock.

The challenge with fresh mallow is the washing, drying, and picking over of the leaves to remove all the stems and any thick or stringy bits. If you can't find fresh, check out Middle Eastern grocery stores for frozen leafy *molokhiya*. It won't be quite the same, but it might give you a taste for these lip-smacking greens.

Makes: about 8 servings

2 tablespoons pine nuts, or sliced almonds
500 g (1 lb 2 oz) whole skinless, boneless chicken breasts
1 teaspoon black pepper
12 garlic cloves, 8 minced and 4 whole
3 tablespoons ghee, or olive oil
1 small onion, diced
2 cardamom pods
2 bay leaves
Small bunch cilantro
Salt and pepper
2 kg (4 ½ lbs) fresh mallow, washed, drained, and stems removed
1 teaspoon ground coriander

Time: 45 minutes

Toast the pine nuts or almonds in a dry skillet over a medium heat for a couple of minutes. Set aside.

Season the chicken breasts with the black pepper, and 2 minced garlic cloves.

In a large sauté pan, heat 1 tablespoon of the ghee. Add the diced onion and two more minced garlic cloves and fry until lightly softened (about 5 minutes). Add the chicken breasts and pan-fry until they have some color on all sides (about 10 minutes). Add 3 cups hot water and the cardamom, bay leaves and cilantro, stalks and all, and season with salt and pepper. Let it come to the boil, remove any froth from the top, then simmer uncovered on a low heat for about 20 minutes, until the chicken is cooked. Lift out the chicken and set it aside, and strain the cooking liquid into a bowl.

Meanwhile, cut 4 whole garlic cloves in half lengthwise. In a large pot, heat 1 tablespoon ghee and sauté the garlic halves, stirring, for a couple of minutes until slightly softened. Add all of the mallow leaves to the pan; you'll probably have to wait for one batch to wilt before adding more. Once all of it is cooked down, season with salt and pepper, add 250 ml (1 cup) of the chicken cooking liquid, cover, and simmer for about 10 minutes.

In a small pan, sauté the remaining 4 minced garlic cloves in the last tablespoon of ghee for a couple of minutes, then add the ground coriander and stir. As the mixture sizzles, tip it over the mallow and stir to combine.

Slice each chicken breast into 3–4 pieces and add it to the mallow. Remove from the heat and pile into a serving dish, sprinkling the toasted pine nuts or almonds on the top.

Chicken Livers with Pomegranate Molasses

 paleo   protein-packed

We keep a pack of chicken livers in the freezer so that whenever we're in a hurry and need a comforting dish, we can just reach in and grab them. We always rinse them in water with a little white vinegar and salt (not too much, as the vinegar tends to "cook" the meat a bit), and they defrost in minutes. In as little as 20 minutes, we can have a delicious home-cooked dish on the table; our family favorites to accompany it are sweet potato wedges or a mound of nutty freekeh. Livers are one of those healthy protein sources, full of vitamin B12 for the brain and iron for the immune system, and therefore highly recommended for kids and adults alike.

Makes: 4–5 servings

1 kg (2 ¼ lb) chicken livers
Salt and pepper
4 garlic cloves, minced
2 tablespoons olive oil
4 tablespoons pomegranate
   molasses
Handful of parsley, stems
   removed and finely chopped
2 tablespoons pomegranate
   seeds (optional)

Time: 20 minutes

Pat the washed livers dry with kitchen paper and sprinkle with black pepper. Place a large sauté pan on a medium-high heat, add the olive oil, and fry the garlic for a minute. Make sure the pan is sizzling hot before adding the chicken liver pieces, to seal in their moisture. Sauté, stirring, until they have some color on all sides (about 5–6 minutes).

Add the pomegranate molasses and sprinkle over some salt, to taste.

Bring to a simmer, then lower the heat, cover, and let the molasses cook the livers for another 5 minutes. Serve hot, garnished with the parsley and pomegranate seeds

Herby Turkey Burgers in Lettuce Wraps

 gluten-free   paleo   protein-packed

Turkey meat is a great source of low-fat protein, but it can be a little bland. This simple recipe packs it with flavor from fresh herbs and greens, and if you cook the burgers on a griddle or barbecue, you'll get that extra dimension from the charring too. Because it's such a low-fat meat mix, the patties need chilling before cooking to firm them up, so it's fine to make them a day in advance and refrigerate them overnight. We use lettuce leaves to wrap the burgers instead of buns to add crunch without the stodge, but we stick with tradition for the sides and relishes, so pile on the tahini sauce, mustard, pickles, tomatoes, and fried onions, and indulge!

Makes: 6 patties

1 onion, cut into chunks
2 garlic cloves
10 basil leaves
1 tablespoon finely chopped thyme
1 tablespoon finely chopped rosemary
½ cup finely chopped parsley
300 g (10.5 oz) finely chopped spinach (about1 ½ cups)
Zest of 1 lime
1 teaspoon sea salt
½ teaspoon black pepper
400 g (14 oz) turkey, minced or diced
2 tablespoons extra-virgin olive oil
1 iceberg lettuce
Pinch of paprika

Time: 30 minutes + 1 hour to chill

Put the onion and garlic into a food processor and pulse until finely chopped. Add the basil, thyme, rosemary, spinach, lime zest, salt and pepper, and pulse to mix. Add the turkey and pulse for a couple of minutes until all is well combined.

Form the mix into burger patties, and place them in the fridge for at least an hour.

To cook the burgers, heat a griddle pan over a medium heat. Brush the burgers with olive oil and cook them on both sides, until firm and browned (about 8 minutes each side).

Separate out whole leaves from the lettuce and toss them in a bowl with the paprika and some salt and pepper.

To serve the perfect wraps, let everyone place a patty in the middle of a lettuce leaf, add their accompaniments of choice, bring the leaf sides over the top to make a neat parcel, and enjoy!

Cinnamon and Pomegranate Molasses Roasted Quails

السمان المشوي بالقرفة ودبس الرمان

 gluten-free   paleo   protein-packed

Quail dishes originate from the Middle East, so it's not surprising to have several recipes with generous spicing to bring out the best in these tasty game birds. To warming cinnamon and allspice we add pomegranate molasses and lime to create a lovely sweet-sour flavor balance that makes the dish rich-tasting without being heavy. We enjoy this dish mostly in the summer when it is the migrating season for the birds. With each person getting a whole, glistening bird, this is a great recipe for an intimate dinner party, especially as all the preparation can be done in advance.

Makes: 4 servings

4 quails
2 red onions, thinly sliced
2 garlic cloves, minced
1 teaspoon ground cinnamon
1 teaspoon allspice
Salt and pepper, to taste
Zest of 2 limes
4 tablespoons olive oil
3 tablespoons pomegranate
  molasses
2 cinnamon sticks
½ cup pomegranate seeds, to
  garnish.

Time: 30 minutes + 2 hours to marinate

In a large bowl (big enough to hold the 4 birds) mix the onion, garlic, ground cinnamon, allspice, salt and pepper, lime zest, olive oil, and pomegranate molasses. Add the quails and rub the mix all over them.

Cover the bowl with cling film and let the quails marinate for about 2 hours (or overnight) in the fridge.

When you're ready to cook, preheat the oven to 180°C (350°F/Gas mark 4), and line an oven tray with baking parchment.

Lift the quails from the bowl, tapping off—but not discarding—any excess marinade, and place them breast-side down on the oven tray, placing the cinnamon sticks between them. Roast for 20 minutes, but halfway through, turn the quails over and baste them with the remaining marinade. When the quails are done, sprinkle over the pomegranate seeds, and serve.

Moroccan Lamb Shoulder

 protein-packed   ⊗ paleo

Rich in protein, B vitamins, zinc, and iron, lamb has a place in a healthy diet. It helps prevent anemia and regular moderate consumption is encouraged for building muscle and heightening athletic performance. This recipe is so much more than protein-packed, however—it incorporates fruits and veggies for fiber and detoxing spices to create a filling, wholesome dish. The lamb shoulder is slowly cooked into tender and delicious bites of joy and the wonderful cooking aromas, warm and fragrant with spices, will draw the whole family to the dining table. Serve it with quinoa, freekeh, or cauliflower rice (see page 128) to mop up every drop of sauce.

Makes: 6–8 servings

For the spice rub:
1 tablespoon ground cumin
2 teaspoons ground coriander
1 teaspoon fennel seeds
1 teaspoon paprika
½ teaspoon chili powder
2 teaspoons salt
½ teaspoon freshly ground black pepper

1 lamb shoulder, bone in (about 1.5 kg/3 lb)
4 tablespoons olive oil
1 large onion, diced
2 cups bone broth (about 500 ml) (see Bone Broth on page 59)
300 g (10.5 oz) cooked chickpeas (about 1 ½ cups) (see Hummus on page 19 for cooking instructions)
1 cup dried apricots, halved
3 large tomatoes, diced
2 cinnamon sticks
1 tablespoon peeled and grated fresh ginger
Zest of one lime
1 tablespoon honey
2 tablespoons finely chopped cilantro, to garnish
A handful of almonds, halved and toasted, to garnish.

Time: 3 hours + marinating time

Mix the ingredients for the spice rub together in a bowl and rub the mixture into the lamb shoulder, coating it well all over. Put it in the fridge for at least 6 hours (or overnight).

When you're ready to cook, heat 2 tablespoons of the olive oil in a large skillet or heavy-bottomed pan over a medium-high heat. Brown the lamb, turning occasionally, on all sides (about 8 minutes).

Transfer the lamb to a plate, turn the heat down to medium, and add the onions to the pan, sautéing for about 5 minutes, until softened. Add the broth, chickpeas, apricots, tomatoes, cinnamon sticks, ginger, lime zest, and honey. Stir to combine and bring to the boil, scraping up any browned bits left from the lamb into the sauce.

Return the lamb to the pan, reduce the heat to low, and cover. Simmer for about 1 ½ hours, until the lamb is tender. Remove the lid and simmer, uncovered, until the sauce is thick enough to coat a spoon (about 20 minutes). Adjust the seasoning, if necessary.

Transfer the lamb and sauce to a serving dish. Sprinkle with the chopped coriander and toasted almonds, and serve.

Sea Salt Roast Beef

 protein-packed   paleo

Cold roast beef is such a versatile food to have in the fridge. Whether cut thick for supper or a hearty sandwich, or wafer-thin for an appetizer or buffet plate, it always delivers on protein power and deliciousness. Most packaged sliced beef is heavily processed, salted and full of preservatives; home-cooked is way tastier, as well as being so much better for you. Here we share our family roast beef recipe, and the way we like to serve it: as a gorgeous, generous platter full of arugula and sea salt and good quality Dijon mustard on the side, for gatherings that will never fail to impress.

Makes: 8–10 servings

250 ml (1 cup) olive oil
125 ml (½ cup) balsamic vinegar
4 tablespoons Dijon mustard
2 teaspoons coarsely ground
   black pepper
4 sprigs of rosemary, stems
   removed and finely chopped
2 kg (4 ½ lb) beef tenderloin,
   trimmed of excess fat
Bunch of arugula, stems
   removed, for serving
2 tablespoons coarse sea salt, for
   serving

Time: 45 minutes + marinating time + 24 hours resting when cooked

Set aside two tablespoons of the olive oil, and put the rest in a small bowl together with the balsamic vinegar, mustard, black pepper, and rosemary.

Rub the mixture all over the beef fillet, working it into every nook and cranny. Put the fillet in the fridge for at least 30 minutes (or overnight) to marinate.

Remove the beef from the fridge half an hour before roasting, so it comes up to room temperature first.

When you're ready to cook, preheat the oven to 200°C (400°F / Gas Mark 6). Heat 2 tablespoons of the olive oil in a large skillet, then brown the beef on all sides (about 10 minutes).

Transfer the fillet to an oven dish, cover with kitchen foil, and roast in the oven for 40 minutes, until fully cooked.

Remove from the oven and lift the fillet out of the dish and onto baking parchment, and wrap it up tightly (tie it up like a parcel if it helps). Once it's cooled down, put it in the fridge for at least 24 hours.

When you're ready to serve, cover a wooden board or large platter with a layer of arugula. Then slice the beef very thin and lay the slices over the leaves. Sprinkle over the coarse salt and some more chopped rosemary, and serve at room temperature.

Beef Casserole with Baby Carrots and Pickled Onions

 protein-packed   paleo

Every Middle Eastern family has their own, treasured recipe for a beef stew. Some home cooks slow-cook the meat with veggies in a rich broth on top of the stove; others pan-fry the spiced meat with sliced onions first, and then place it in the oven. This recipe is in the latter camp; it's full of flavorful spices that percolate into the meat while it slow-cooks in the oven. The beef comes out wonderfully tender, while the carrots melt in your mouth. However, it's the pickled onions that make this dish so special for us: they just deepen and enrich the meaty flavors while also adding some bright, sweet notes. (But you can substitute fresh onions if you like.) As the meat will be cooked long and slow, you can use something economical like chuck steak or rump, but if you need to keep the fat content down, choose a leaner cut. We serve this stew with freekeh, to soak up all the yummy gravy.

Makes: 4 servings

600 g (1.3 lb) boneless beef chuck or shin of beef, cut into 3 cm (1.2 in) cubes
1 tablespoon coarse black pepper
2 teaspoon allspice
2–3 tablespoons coconut oil
2 garlic cloves, minced
15 baby pickled onions
300 g (10.5 oz) baby or slender carrots
60 ml (¼ cup) pickled onion liquid (optional)
1 cinnamon stick
3–4 cloves
2 bay leaves

Time: 2 ½ hours + marinating time

Pat the meat dry with kitchen paper, then sprinkle over the black pepper and allspice, turning until all the pieces are covered. Refrigerate for 30 minutes to marinate.

When you're ready to cook, preheat the oven to 180°C (350°F/Gas mark 4).

Heat the coconut oil in a Dutch oven or heavy-bottomed casserole on a medium heat. Sauté the garlic for a minute then add the pickled onions and carrots (halve any very large ones), and stir for a few minutes. Season with salt and pepper.

Make sure the pan is hot, then add the beef and brown it, stirring occasionally to lightly brown each side of each piece. Drizzle in more oil if needed.

Once browned, drizzle over the pickled onion liquid (if using), and scrape the sides and base of the pan to get all the flavorful bits stuck to the pan into your sauce.

Add 2 cups hot water, the cinnamon stick, cloves, and bay leaves, and bring to a boil. Cover the pan and place in the middle of the oven for about 2 hours. About 30 minutes before it's ready, stir to remove anything sticking to the sides. Replace the cover and put it back in the oven.

Before serving, discard the cinnamon stick, cloves, and bay leaves if you wish.

Maqluba Freekeh

مقلوبة فريك باللحمة والباذنجان

 protein-packed   ⊗ paleo

Maqluba, which means "upside down," is a dish in which meat, vegetables, and rice are layered in a large pot which is then inverted onto a serving platter to reveal a gorgeous, savory mountain of good things. The "ta-dah!" moment when the pan is lifted away brings cheers from family and friends at any homey gathering.

We make our maqluba with hearty beef, succulent eggplant, and freekeh rather than traditional rice, which tastes so much better with its light sweetness and is full of protein.

Makes: 8–10 servings

750 g (1 ½ lb) boneless beef chuck or shin of beef cut into 3–4 cm (roughly 1.5 in) cubes
2 tablespoons black pepper
1 tablespoon allspice
2 tablespoons ghee or olive oil
2 cinnamon sticks
4 bay leaves
4 cardamom pods
4 cloves
Salt
2 tablespoons olive oil
2 large eggplants, cut into 2.5 cm (1 in) cubes
Half a cauliflower, cut into small florets (about 2 cups)
500 g (1 lb 2 oz) freekeh (about 2 ½ cups)
Good handful of cooked chickpeas (see Hummus on page 19 for cooking instructions)
Handful of parsley leaves, roughly chopped to garnish

Time: 3 hours

Put the beef into a bowl, sprinkle over the black pepper and allspice, and mix with your hands.

Heat the ghee or olive oil in a large casserole or Dutch oven. Sauté the beef cubes until they have some color on all sides but are not cooked through (about 12 minutes).

Add 1.5 liters (6 cups) hot water, 1 cinnamon stick, 2 bay leaves, 2 cardamom pods, 2 cloves and a sprinkling of salt. Stir and simmer, covered, on low heat for about 1 hour, then uncovered for another 15 minutes to evaporate some of the liquid.

In the meantime, preheat the oven to 180°C (350°F/Gas mark 4). Line an oven tray with baking parchment, and brush with olive oil. Spread the eggplant and cauliflower on the tray, drizzle with olive oil and season with salt and pepper. Roast for about 15 minutes, flipping the vegetables halfway through.

To assemble the maqluba, use a large, round soup pan. With a slotted spoon, lift the meat out of its cooking broth (keep the broth!) and set it in the pan. Press the meat down into a firm, well-packed layer. Follow with the eggplant and cauliflower, pressing them down into an even layer.

Ladle a little of the cooking broth over the vegetables. Tip the washed freekeh over the top and level it. Set the pot back on the stove top over a low heat.

Maqluba Freekeh (cont.)

To the remaining cooking broth, add 3 cups hot water, season with salt and pepper, and add the remaining cinnamon stick, 2 bay leaves, 2 cardamom pods, and 2 cloves. Stir, scraping up any residue clinging to the sides and bottom of the pan into the broth. Bring to a simmer, uncovered, to reduce for 5 minutes.

Pour the hot broth with spices slowly over the freekeh so it doesn't float (you want the liquid to rise up from the bottom of the pan into it, not splash over the top) until it's just covered, by about a finger's width. If you need more liquid, add water from a boiling kettle. Cover the pot and let it cook for 30 minutes, or until the freekeh is cooked through. In the last 5 minutes, lay a round plate over the freekeh inside the pan and press down on it here and there to eliminate any air pockets within the dish (you might see bubbles rise and pop, which is what you want).

Remove the pan from the heat and let it rest for a few minutes. Remove the plate.

Place a large round, shallow serving dish face down over the pot. Holding the dish and pan together, flip the whole thing over. Set it down, dish at the bottom, and leave for a couple of minutes to make sure all the ingredients have fallen off the bottom of the pan. Lift off the pan, scatter over the chickpeas and parsley, and serve immediately.

Slow-cooked Veal Shanks

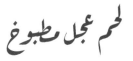

 protein-packed   paleo

This, the casserole that the Italians call *osso buco*, is comfort food at its yummiest, the type of juicy, tender, slow-cooked, falling-off-the-bone meat dish that soothes the soul while delivering a wow factor on flavor. Don't be intimidated by the number of ingredients; while the cooked dish will look and taste impressively sophisticated, the recipe itself is really simple.

Traditionally *osso buco* is made with veal shanks, but we've also made this with neck, another economical cut; in both cases, your butcher will be able to cut it into thick steaks, each with a marrow-filled bone at its center. Ask, also, if they will tie each piece around the circumference to make sure the meat doesn't fall off the bones. It doesn't affect the taste, but it makes the finished dish look super special.

Makes: 6 servings

2 kg (4 ½ lb) veal shanks or neck
1 tablespoon garlic powder
2 tablespoons black pepper
1 teaspoon ground nutmeg
2 tablespoons olive oil
2 tablespoons ghee, or coconut oil
4 stalks celery, diced
2 green onions, chopped
4 carrots, diced
Juice of 2 limes
2 sprigs thyme, finely chopped
2 sprigs rosemary, finely chopped
2 bay leaves
Salt
1 kg (2 ¼ lb) tomatoes, peeled and puréed (about 2–3 cups)
1 lime zest
2 tablespoons parsley leaves, roughly chopped for garnish

Time: 2 hours + marinating time

Season the veal with the garlic powder, black pepper, and nutmeg, rubbing them into the meat. Marinate in fridge, covered, for 30 minutes.

In a large, heavy-bottomed pan, heat the olive oil and ghee on a medium heat. Brown the meat on each side (about 5 minutes); you'll probably need to do this in batches.

In the same hot pan, add the diced vegetables and lime juice and sauté for a few minutes until the celery and onion take on some color. Then add the rosemary and thyme and stir. Add the puréed tomatoes and bay leaves, and season the sauce generously with salt and pepper. Stir, scraping the bottom of the pan and the sides.

When it starts to bubble, reduce the heat to medium-low, put the meat back in the pan, spooning sauce over all the pieces, and cover. Cook for up to 90 minutes, or until meat is tender and the sauce has darkened. If about halfway through, you feel the sauce has thickened a lot but the meat is not cooked through, add some hot water, scraping in the bits stuck to the pan.

To serve, lift the shanks out, remove any string, and place on a large serving dish. Ladle the vegetable-rich sauce over the meat, sprinkle on lime zest and some parsley leaves, and serve hot.

Eggplant Ground-meat Boats

باذنجان باللحمة المفرومة والجوز

 protein-packed   paleo

Such a warm dish from the heart of the Middle East, these individual moussaka-style boats are made with fresh tomatoes, ground beef, and a touch of pomegranate molasses that brings sweetness into the savory equation. Our kids love the little ships with their walnut "captains" that are comforting and delicious with lots of different tastes and textures. Any leftovers are delicious cold the next day.

Eggplant, a "nightshade" food, can't be eaten by those on some strict anti-inflammatory diets, but zucchini or other summer squash can be good substitutes in this recipe.

Makes: 8 boats

4 medium eggplants, of roughly
    the same size
3 tablespoons olive oil
Salt and pepper
1 onion, diced
4 garlic cloves
250 g (9 oz) ground beef
½ teaspoon cinnamon
1 large tomato, diced
1 tablespoon pomegranate
    molasses
Handful of raisins
2 medium tomatoes, puréed with
    60 ml (¼ cup) water
Handful of walnuts

Time: 45 minutes

Halve the eggplants lengthways to make the boat shape. Cut and scoop out the inner flesh, leaving a firm shell. Roughly chop the scooped-out flesh and set aside. Brush the shells generously with olive oil on all sides, season with salt and pepper, and set aside.

Preheat the oven to 180°C (350°F/Gas mark 4).

In a large pan, heat the olive oil and sauté the onions and garlic for a few minutes. Add the scooped-out eggplant flesh and cook for a few more minutes, then add the ground beef, cinnamon, and salt and pepper. Stir occasionally until the mix is cooked through (about 10 minutes).

Stir in the diced tomato, raisins, and a drizzle of pomegranate molasses and cook for another 5 minutes.

Pour the puréed tomatoes into a large oven dish. This layer of liquid will help cook the eggplant boats through in the oven. Fill each eggplant boat with about 3 tablespoons of the ground meat mix, place a walnut on top of each, and arrange them next to each other in the oven dish.

Place the dish in the middle of the oven for 25 minutes, until the eggplants are cooked through and the walnuts are browned and toasted.

Chargrill-flavor Kofta

 protein-packed   paleo

This ground-meat recipe is hardly new for a Middle Eastern cook, or a non-local. But this is the yummiest, most moist Kofta recipe . . . with a trick! One that will give you that barbecue flavor you can't quite achieve in the oven.

Here, we heat a piece of charcoal and place it in the pan with the meat, just like our grandmother did. It will be the best thing that happened to your kofta and to your family dinners.

Of course, and this is important, make sure you are using natural non-toxic charcoal.

Makes: 12–14

500 g ground meat (preferably beef)
Small bunch of parsley, chopped (about ½ cup)
Small handful of cilantro, chopped
Small handful of mint, chopped
2 garlic cloves, finely minced
1 teaspoon ground cumin
1 teaspoon ground coriander
1 teaspoon paprika
½ teaspoon ground cinnamon
1 egg
Salt and pepper
Drizzle of olive oil
1 large onion

Time: 45 minutes

Preheat the oven to 180°C (350°F/Gas mark 4).

Put the ground meat and onion into a large bowl. Add the herbs and spices, then crack the egg over all the ingredients. Season with salt and pepper. Mix well with your hands.

Form the mix into kofta-shaped fingers and lay them side by side in a large oven-proof pan, preferably one with a lid. Place them, uncovered, in the oven for 25 minutes, turning halfway through.

As they cook, place a piece of non-toxic charcoal straight on the stove to start burning. This should take about 5 minutes.

In the meantime, use a knife to remove the middle of a large onion, leaving the outer layer shaped like a small bowl. When the kofta are cooked, take the pan out of the oven and place on a heat-proof surface. Make a space in the center of the pan and place the onion, open side up, in the middle. Using tongs, very carefully fetch the burning charcoal and put it in the onion bowl. Cover the pan immediately, either with the lid or tightly with foil (making sure the foil doesn't come in contact with the meat).

Leave for a few minutes to rest and absorb the smoky flavor, then remove the cover and the coal, and serve the kofta warm, juicy, and smelling fabulous.

To dispose of the burning coal, immerse it in some water to stop it burning before throwing it away.

From the Sea اسماك

Baked Whole Fish with Tahini and Coriander

 protein-packed   paleo

All around the Mediterranean, fish is sold fresh and in abundance straight off the beach. As we spend most of our days swimming or chilling, we don't want to spend too much time cooking, nor eat anything too heavy. This delicious fish dish is easy and quick to prepare. If you can't find a sea bass or bream big enough to feed four, then use two medium-sized fish; you can even use fillets, tucking the flavorings under and over them—but keep the cooking time down to 20 minutes maximum.

A tahini dip is a traditional side for fish feasts in the Middle East; here we use tahini in a sauce for the baked fish, adding flavor and substance to the dish.

Makes: 4 servings

1 whole, cleaned sea bass or sea bream, about 1.5 kg/3 lb in weight
2 tablespoons olive oil
Juice of 3 limes (about ½ cup)
1 large onion, thinly sliced
1 tablespoon pomegranate molasses
1 lemon (or 2 limes), thinly sliced
1 bunch cilantro
10 garlic cloves, minced
250 ml (1 cup) tahini paste
½ teaspoon chili powder, plus extra to taste
1–2 tablespoons salt, to taste
4 tablespoons ground coriander
1 tablespoon finely chopped parsley, to garnish
2 tablespoons pomegranate seeds, to garnish

Time: 40 minutes

Preheat the oven to 200°C (400°F/Gas Mark 6), and line an oven tray with baking parchment.

Cut parallel, diagonal slits in the skin of the fish on both sides. Rub one tablespoon of the olive oil into the fish skin and the cuts, and sprinkle over a tablespoon of the lime juice.

Sauté the sliced onion in another tablespoon of olive oil for about 7 minutes, until softened, then add the pomegranate molasses and stir for another couple of minutes.

Stuff the fish cavity with the cooked onion mixture, cilantro, and lemon or lime slices. Carefully lift the fish onto the oven tray and put it in the oven for 20–25 minutes.

While the fish bakes, set a medium pan over a medium heat and add to it the garlic, the rest of the lime juice, the tahini, about 2 cups water, salt, coriander, and chili. Mix well while bringing to the boil, then lower the heat and gently simmer, uncovered, until the mix has fully come together as a sauce. If it seems too thick, add a little more water.

Once the fish is baked, lay it out on a serving platter, pour the cooked tahini sauce over it, and garnish with the chopped parsley and pomegranate seeds.

Almond-crusted Sea Bass

 protein-packed   paleo

This is one of our favorite fish recipes, so easy to make but tasting like a million dollars. The crispy coating surrounding the tender bass, with all the goodness of nuts, fresh herbs, and spices, rivals any breaded or battered fish and packs a real flavor punch, too. It's a winning dish for any dinner, especially when served with a green salad and a spiced tahini sauce.

Makes: 4 servings

4 sea bass fillets, about 125 g (4.5 oz) each
150 g (5 oz) raw almonds, peeled
Handful of mint, leaves only, finely chopped
Handful of parsley, stalks removed and finely chopped
Handful of cilantro, stalks removed and finely chopped
2 teaspoons ground cumin
1 teaspoon ground coriander
Pinch of chili powder, or to taste
2 eggs
60 ml (¼ cup) almond milk
Salt and pepper
4 tablespoons olive oil

Time: 20 minutes

In a food processor or coffee mill, grind the almonds into a grainy powder.

Mix the almonds with the chopped herbs and the spices, and spread the mixture out in a layer on a large flat plate.

In a small bowl, whisk the eggs and almond milk together and season with salt and pepper.

Dip a fish fillet into the egg mixture, making sure it coats both sides. Then press each side onto the nut and herb coating until well covered. Repeat with the rest of the fillets.

The fillets are best fried in batches.

Heat two tablespoons of olive oil in a large skillet and add 2 fillets.

Cook them on each side for about 5 minutes until golden. Then cover for another 5 minutes to cook through. Lift the fillets out and place on kitchen paper to absorb any excess oil, and keep warm while you cook the second batch of fish in another 2 tablespoons of olive oil. Once they are done, serve immediately.

White Fish Cakes with Sweet Potato and Herbs

 protein-packed   🌾 gluten-free

Kids who aren't big fish fans usually don't have a problem with fish cakes, and these are a perfect way to get some of those healthy omega-3 oils into their diet. They love the sweet potato, too, and we pack even more nutrients in by adding egg, quinoa, and lots of fresh herbs. We include chili for a flavor lift, but you could always leave it out.

This recipe works really well with cooked leftover white fish from a previous meal. You can also use cooked salmon if you prefer.

Makes: 6 patties

400 g (14 oz) sea bass or bream fillets
Zest and juice of 1 lime
Salt and pepper
Flesh of 2 medium sweet potatoes, baked then mashed
90 g (3 oz) cooked quinoa, preferably red (about ½ cup)
2 green onions, finely chopped
Small bunch of cilantro, stalks removed and finely chopped
Small bunch of parsley, stalks removed and finely chopped
1 teaspoon dried chili flakes
1 tablespoon olive oil
2 eggs, beaten
2 tablespoons coconut oil, for frying

Time: 45 minutes

Preheat the oven to 200°C (400°F/Gas Mark 6).

In an ovenproof dish, season the fish fillets with the lime zest and juice, salt, and pepper and bake for 20 minutes. Set aside to cool.

In a large bowl, stir together the cooked sweet potato with the quinoa, then mix in the rest of the ingredients except the coconut oil. Chop the fish and add it to the mix. Combine well to form a firm mixture, then use your hands to create 6 burger-shaped patties.

Heat the coconut oil in a large pan. Fry the patties for 4 minutes on each side, until browned and crispy. Serve warm, with a salad.

Grilled Shrimp with a Chickpea and Cucumber Salad

 protein-packed   (grain icon) gluten-free

Sizzling, fragrant shrimp are a big favorite with us. We use a good helping of chili, but you can reduce the amount to taste. You need to remove the black "vein" that runs down the curve of the back, which is their digestive tract. Making an incision in the shrimp gives you a little pocket to pack more flavor into, and the shells lock it all in as they cook. We serve them straight off the grill with this hearty, tangy chickpea and cucumber salad.

Makes: 4 generous servings, or 8 as an appetizer

16 large raw shrimp, shell on (about 1 kg/2 ¼ lb)
7 garlic cloves, thinly sliced
3 teaspoons sumac
Salt and pepper
Zest and juice of 2 limes
2 teaspoons dried chili flakes, or to taste
Handful cilantro, stalks removed and finely chopped
2 tablespoons olive oil

For the salad:
1 red onion, halved and thinly sliced
2 tablespoons white vinegar
Handful parsley, stems removed and finely chopped
Handful cilantro, stems removed and finely chopped
2 cucumbers, halved lengthways and sliced
1 large turnip, halved and thinly sliced
400 g (15 oz) cooked chickpeas (see Hummus on page 19 for cooking instructions)
2 tablespoons olive oil
Juice of 2 limes
Salt and pepper

Time: 20 minutes + marinating time

Rinse the shrimp thoroughly under running water and pat dry. With a sharp knife, make an incision along the back of each shrimp, cutting to about halfway through, and use the tip of your knife to pull out and discard the black vein.

Stuff the cut in each shrimp with some of the garlic slices and lime zest, and a pinch each of sumac, salt, and pepper. Place the shrimp in a medium bowl and add the chopped cilantro, chili flakes, and olive oil. Use your hands to mix well, coating the shrimps all over. Put the bowl in the fridge for 30 minutes (they can stay in there longer, even overnight).

Prepare the salad just before you cook the shrimp. Slice the red onion first, and put it in a glass bowl with the vinegar to steep for about 10 minutes, while you prepare the rest of the vegetables.

Drain the onion, and add it to a medium bowl with the chopped herbs, cucumber, turnip, and chickpeas. Drizzle over the olive oil and lime juice, add salt and pepper to taste, and mix well.

Set a large skillet or griddle over medium heat for a minute, then add all the shrimp and the marinade and let them sizzle for 10 minutes, turning them halfway. Watch as the shrimps turn from translucent grey to opaque, then gloriously pink with bright tails when they're cooked. Splash the lime juice over them just before taking off the heat, and serve with the salad.

Ginger Shrimp with Warm Lentils

 protein-packed   paleo

Packed with nutrients and healthy proteins, this is such a filling and heartwarming dish. While shrimp and lentils both feature in Middle Eastern cooking, it's unusual to find them combined. Rice is the more common accompaniment to shrimp, but we find that lentils are just as good—perhaps even better—at soaking up all that seafoody savor, especially when the zesty marinade is added to the cooking.

Makes: 4 servings

500 g (18 oz) medium raw shrimp, tail on
1 teaspoon grated fresh ginger
3 garlic cloves, minced
½ red chili pepper, deseeded and finely chopped
Zest and juice of 2 limes
400 g (15 oz) brown lentils (about 2 cups)
½ teaspoon ground cumin
Salt and pepper
2 tablespoons olive oil
2 green onions, finely chopped
1 tablespoon raisins, optional

Time: 45 minutes

In a medium glass bowl, place the shrimp, ginger, garlic, chili, and lime zest and juice, and mix well to coat the shrimp all over. Cover with plastic film and put in the fridge to marinate while you cook the lentils.

Wash the lentils in a sieve under cold running water. Put them in a medium pan, cover with fresh cold water, and bring to the boil. Stir in the cumin, add salt and pepper, cover, and let simmer for about 25 minutes, or until the lentils are cooked through but not mushy.

Heat the olive oil in a large sauté pan and stir in the green onions.

Using a slotted spoon, lift the shrimp from the bowl and add them to the pan. Let them cook for about 5 minutes, until they turn pink, then add the lentils and the remainder of the marinade liquid. Follow with the raisins, if using any. Adjust the seasoning if needed and give a final stir to combine, then serve hot.

Oven-baked Calamari and Bell Pepper Tagine

طاجن كاليماري بالفلفل الملون

 gluten-free   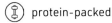 paleo   protein-packed

In any seafood restaurant on the Mediterranean you'll find a squid tagine served in one way or the other. Moroccans spice it with turmeric and saffron, while Italians cook it on the stove with a herbed tomato sauce, then finish it in the oven. We're sharing here a simple recipe that we grew up eating on the famous corniche in Alexandria. In Egypt it's cooked in a traditional clay pot called a bram instead of the cone-shaped North African tagine, but an earthenware oven dish will be fine for this recipe; it doesn't need a lid, as there's no long, slow cooking required. In fact the trick with calamari is not to overcook it; if you're not sure that it's done, always try a piece before deciding to prolong the cooking. You'll usually find that it's already perfect.

We like to serve this tagine with freekeh for a complete nutritional package.

Makes: 4–5 servings

500 g (18 oz) calamari, cut into short strips
1 teaspoon cumin
Pinch of chili powder, or to taste
Salt and pepper
3 tablespoons olive oil
1 onion, sliced into wedges
3 garlic cloves, minced
½ red bell pepper, cut into squares
½ yellow bell pepper, cut into squares
1 tomato, diced
3 tomatoes, peeled and puréed
Handful of parsley, stems removed and finely chopped, to garnish.

Time: 40 minutes + marinating time

Place the calamari in a bowl and add the cumin, chili powder, and salt and pepper, tossing to coat all the strips. Marinate in the fridge for 30 minutes to 2 hours.

To cook, heat 2 tablespoons of olive oil in a sauté pan and fry the onion wedges and garlic for a few minutes, stirring occasionally. Add the peppers and cook for a few minutes before adding the diced tomato. Cook for a couple of minutes more, then transfer it to an oven dish. Set aside.

Preheat the oven to 180°C (350°F/Gas mark 4).

Using the same sauté pan (no need to wash), heat 1 tablespoon of the olive oil, then add the calamari (making sure pan is hot) and cook, stirring, for about 5 minutes. Add the puréed tomato and ¼ cup hot water, season with salt and pepper, then bring to the boil, using a wooden spoon or spatula to scrape the sides and bottom of the pan.

Add the calamari and sauce to the oven dish, and distribute the vegetables and calamari evenly. Bake in the middle of the oven for 15 minutes. Serve hot, sprinkled with the freshly chopped parsley.

Grilled Calamari with Pomegranate Molasses and Chili

 paleo   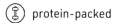 protein-packed

Another omega-3-rich recipe, perfect for summer days by the sea. It is light (squid is very low in saturated fat), sweet, and tangy. We prepare it at our beach getaway as part of a bigger seafood feast or a mezze dish. Either way, the combination of ingredients is delicious and so good for you.

Makes: mezze for 4

250 g (9 oz) calamari, cut into strips of equal size
½ teaspoon ground cumin
Salt and pepper
2 tablespoons olive oil
2 garlic cloves, minced
½ teaspoon dried chili flakes or chili powder, or to taste
1 green onion, white part only, finely sliced
3 tablespoons pomegranate molasses
2 tablespoons water
Lime wedges, for serving

Time: 25 minutes

In a bowl, mix the calamari with the cumin, season with salt and pepper, and place in the fridge for 15 minutes or so to soak up the flavors.

When you're ready to cook, set a large griddle or sauté pan on a medium to high heat; once it's hot, add to it the olive oil, minced garlic, and chili flakes. Let them fry for a minute, then add the green onions and calamari.

Fry the calamari on all sides for about 5 minutes. Add the pomegranate molasses and water and let it cook through for another 3 minutes. Don't overcook the calamari, or they will be chewy. Try a piece, and adjust the seasoning if necessary. Serve as soon as ready, with fresh lime wedges to squeeze over it.

Freekeh Paella

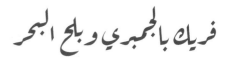

فريك بالجمبري وبلح البحر

(icon) protein-packed

No, paella isn't a traditional dish in our part of the world, but we've found that we can use our Middle Eastern super grain, freekeh, to make a fantastic version that's so good, and so good for you, that we had to share it. Nutritionally, it knocks spots off a paella made with refined white rice.

This feast of seafood flavors needs your largest frying pan or, better, one of the big, purpose-made paella pans. With one of these, you could double up the quantities for a lunch or supper party. Although it's basically a one-pot recipe, this colorful dish always looks so special and festive, especially if you let your guests help themselves to their favorite morsels. You'll likely find them sidling up to the pan for seconds.

Makes: 6 large servings

300 g (10.5 oz) freekeh (about 1½ cups)
2 tablespoons olive oil
1 large onion, diced
½ red bell pepper, diced
½ yellow bell pepper, diced
10 garlic cloves, minced
1 large tomato, finely diced
½ teaspoon saffron
½ teaspoon chili powder, or to taste
Salt and pepper
1 liter (4 cups) hot fish or vegetable stock, or water
200 g (7 oz) calamari, sliced
1 cup fresh (or frozen) peas
250 g (9 oz) clams
250 g (9 oz) mussels
6 jumbo shell-on shrimp, deveined and rinsed
½ teaspoon garlic powder
Handful of parsley, stalks removed and finely chopped, to garnish
2 lemons cut into wedges, to garnish

Time: 40 minutes

Wash the freekeh in a sieve under cold running water, and set aside to drain.

Set a large skillet or paella pan over a medium heat, and drizzle in the olive oil. Add the diced onions, peppers, and garlic, and sauté until tender.

Add the diced tomato and saffron, and half the chili, salt, and pepper to taste, and cook for one more minute. Add the washed freekeh, and stir until all is well combined.

Add the warm stock (or water), the calamari, and the peas. When the liquid starts to bubble, reduce the heat, cover, and let simmer for about 20 minutes until the freekeh is tender and the liquid has been absorbed.

While the pan simmers, season the clams, mussels, and shrimp with salt, pepper, the remaining chili, and garlic powder.

When the 20 minutes are up, take off the lid, arrange the shrimp, clams, and mussels on top of the paella, replace the lid and continue to cook for 8–10 more minutes, until the clams and mussels have opened (discard any that have stayed closed) and the shrimp have turned pink. Garnish with fresh chopped parsley and lemon wedges, and serve.

Sweet Things الحلو

Avo-chocolate Mousse with Fresh Pomegranate

 vegan   gluten-free

Who said vegans can't enjoy a chocolate mousse? Let alone one that's brimful of nutrients and feel-good deliciousness. The creaminess of this mousse is provided by avocados, but don't let that put you off: their flavor is masked by the cocoa and molasses. We serve it to our kids and girlfriends all the time (it only takes 15 minutes to prepare) and they never guess how healthy and good for them it is. To serve, we add pomegranate seeds and a touch of mint to balance the smooth richness with some crunchy freshness, but you can play around with it as you wish—try garnishing instead with toasted nuts or coconut flakes.

Makes: 4 large servings

2 ripe avocados, peeled and cut into chunks
4 tablespoons raw molasses
5 tablespoons cocoa powder
1 teaspoon vanilla extract
Pinch of salt
Seeds from one medium-sized pomegranate (around ¾ cup)
8–10 mint leaves

Time: 15 minutes

Finely chop half of the mint leaves. Reserve a spoonful of the pomegranate seeds and put the rest, with the chopped mint, into a bowl; add one tablespoon of the molasses and stir to combine. Place in the fridge until the chocolate mousse is ready.

In a food processor bowl, put the avocado chunks, the rest of the molasses, the cocoa powder, vanilla extract, and pinch of salt. Pulse until completely smooth and creamy. You might need to stop once or twice to scrape the sides of the bowl down.

To serve, tip all of the pomegranate mixture into a large bowl and spoon the chocolate mousse over it, then garnish with the remaining mint leaves and pomegranate seeds. Alternatively, layer the mixture in four individual serving dishes.

Date and Tahini Cups

 vegan

Peanut butter cups face serious competition here. We just love this combination of tahini, dates, and chocolate, and we think you will, too.

We always use Mejdoul dates for preference, although you could use fresh soft black dates. You could also substitute raw honey for the molasses.

These cups will keep well in the freezer (ideal for when you need a quick sweet fix) or, once they are set, in the fridge for up to five days.

Makes: 8-9 cups

For the base:
12 large dates, pitted
60 g (2 oz) oats
60 g (2 oz) walnuts

For the center:
225 g (8 oz) tahini paste (about 1 cup)
4-5 tablespoons raw molasses
2 large dates, pitted
Pinch of salt

For the topping:
3 tablespoons coconut oil
2 tablespoons raw cocoa powder
1 tablespoon raw molasses

Time: 90 minutes

To prepare the base, place the 12 dates in a food processor with a tablespoon of water. Pulse until you have a creamy mixture. Add the oats and walnuts and pulse again until combined.

Place 9 paper cupcake liners in a muffin pan, or just brush it with coconut oil. Press down about 1 ½ tablespoons of the date-oat dough in each to form the bases of the cups, and place in the freezer for 15 minutes.

In the meantime, use the food processor to mix the ingredients for the center together (the tahini, raw molasses, 2 dates, and salt).

When you remove the bases from the freezer, spread a tablespoon or two of this mix over each, and pop back in the freezer for another 15 minutes.

In a medium bowl, mix the ingredients for the topping together. Remove the tray of cups from the freezer, spread the topping mix over each, and put back in the freezer for another hour to set.

Spiced Brown Rice Pudding

حلو الأرز البني ودبس البلح

⊘ vegan   ✿ gluten-free

Every grandmother in the Middle East has her own rice pudding recipe, held sacred within the family. As delicious as most of these heirloom recipes are, they inevitably rely on dairy and sugar. Here we give you a vegan, naturally sweetened version that lies somewhere between a tweak and a reinvention. Aromatic, spiced, and sweet, our kids tested it and loved it. Give it a try and it'll become your staple comfort dessert.

Makes: 4–6 servings

285 g (10 oz) brown rice (about 1 ½ cups)
400 ml (14 fl oz or 1 can) coconut milk
Pinch of salt
4 sprigs thyme
2 cardamom pods
2 cinnamon sticks
4–5 cloves
4–5 tablespoons date molasses, or raw molasses
Handful chopped toasted almonds or walnuts, raisins, or sliced bananas (optional)

Time: 30 minutes

Wash the brown rice well in a sieve under running water.

Put the coconut milk, 1 cup water, salt, and spices in a medium saucepan. Bring to the boil over a high heat.

Add the rice to the saucepan, cover, and lower the heat to a simmer. Stir the rice occasionally to make sure it doesn't stick at the bottom. The rice should be cooked and sticky in about 25 minutes.

Stir in the molasses then remove the pan from the heat. Remove the cinnamon sticks, cardamom pods, cloves, and thyme sprigs. Serve warm in individual bowls, or put it in the fridge to cool first. An extra drizzle of molasses, sliced bananas, chopped almonds, walnuts, and raisins all make good garnishes.

Tahini Chocolate Squares

 كيك الشوكورا تة بالطحينة

 gluten-free   (paleo) paleo   (I) protein-packed

Brownies step aside! These sugar-free, dairy-free, guilt-free tahini and molasses chocolate squares are amazingly delicious and full of wholesome ingredients, perfect to satisfy that sweet craving or as a post-workout snack. Tahini and raw molasses are a match made in heaven. Tahini provides the creamy lusciousness while molasses is a light sweetener, full of iron and vitamins. The eggs and the healthy fats in almond flour ensure that these treats turn out moist and gooey. Eat them warm with your coffee, or keep in the fridge for up to a week

Makes: 9 squares

115 g (4 oz) tahini paste (about ½ cup)
140 g (5oz) raw molasses (about ½ cup)
2 eggs
1 teaspoon vanilla extract
60 g (2 oz) almond flour
1 teaspoon baking powder
30 g cocoa powder (about ¼ cup)
Pinch of salt
2 tablespoons dark chocolate chips (optional)

For the tahini ganache topping:
1 ½ tablespoons tahini paste
2 tablespoons raw molasses
1 teaspoon cocoa powder

Time: 20 minutes

Preheat the oven to 180°C (350°F/Gas mark 4). Line a square, 20 by 20 cm (8 by 8 in) baking pan or dish with baking parchment. Dust with some almond flour to prevent the dough sticking to the paper.

Put the tahini, raw molasses, eggs, and vanilla extract in a medium bowl. Whisk to combine before slowly adding the almond flour, baking powder, and cocoa powder. Sprinkle in a pinch of salt. Combine the mixture into a creamy, slightly sticky dough.

Spread the dough in the pan and, if using, distribute the chocolate chips evenly over the top. Place in the middle of the oven for 15 minutes, until baked through but still somewhat soft.

While the cake mix bakes, prepare the tahini ganache topping by mixing all the ingredients together well. Set aside.

When the cake is done, remove from the oven and let it cool for about 15 minutes. Remove it from the pan and place it upside down so as to slowly unpeel the baking parchment from the bottom. Then place it on a cutting board.

Spread with the tahini ganache then cut into 9 equal-sized squares.

Spiced Date and Nut Cake

 protein-packed

This is a warming bake for cool autumn days when you want something mildly sweet and comforting with your coffee, or to pop in the kids' lunchboxes. Full of nutritious bananas, dates, almonds, walnuts, and spices, it's our go-to cake recipe for family, friends, and school functions.

Makes: around 8 slices

3 ripe bananas, roughly chopped
125 ml (½ cup) almond milk
125 ml (½ cup) raw honey (or date molasses for vegans)
1 teaspoon vanilla extract
125 ml (½ cup) coconut oil, melted or olive oil, plus 1 tablespoon for brushing
115 g (4 oz) almond flour (about 1 cup)
115 g (4 oz) brown rice flour (about 1 cup), plus extra for dusting
2 teaspoons baking powder
2 teaspoons baking soda
2 teaspoons ground cinnamon
Pinch of nutmeg
Pinch of salt
8 large dates, preferably Medjoul, pitted and diced
30 g (1 oz) walnuts, roughly chopped
2 tablespoons pumpkin seeds (optional)
2 tablespoons raw or date molasses (optional)

Time: 50 minutes

Preheat the oven to 180°C (350°F/Gas mark 4). Line a 22 cm (8 in) round cake pan with baking parchment and brush with melted coconut oil or olive oil.

In a mixing bowl, place the bananas, almond milk, honey, and vanilla extract. Use a handheld mixer to combine into a smooth consistency. Slowly add the melted coconut or olive oil while beating.

In another bowl, mix the almond and rice flour, baking powder, baking soda, cinnamon, nutmeg, and salt.

Slowly add the dry ingredients to the wet ingredients as you continue to beat.

When the batter is completely smooth and combined, dust the diced dates and walnuts in a little flour then fold them into the batter with a spatula or spoon. The flour coating will stop them sinking to the bottom of the cake in the oven.

Tip the batter into the cake pan, shake the pan to level it and, if using, sprinkle the pumpkin seeds on top.

Bake in the middle of the oven for 30–35 minutes, or until a knife tip inserted into the middle comes out clean.

As soon as the cake comes out of the oven, if you want an extra sweet crust, brush the molasses all over the top. Then, give the cake a few minutes to rest before you remove it from the pan.

Walnut and Seed Energy Balls

 vegan  gluten-free   protein-packed

These treats are not just a great pick-me-up on busy days but also oh, so delicious, with their earthy walnut flavor and chewy date and tahini centers coated with a crunch of toasted sesame. You could also use toasted coconut or cocoa powder to coat the balls, if you prefer. Perfect for kids' lunchboxes or a post-workout snack, they'll keep in the fridge for up to a week.

Makes: around 20 balls

225 g (8 oz) walnuts (about 2 cups)
2 tablespoons flax seeds
20 dates, preferably Medjoul, pitted
115 g (4 oz) tahini paste (about ½ cup)
115 g (4 oz) raw or date molasses (about 5 tablespoons)
70 g (2 ½ oz) sesame seeds (about ½ cup)

Time: 10 minutes

Put the walnuts and flax seeds into a food processor, and pulse until you have a rough powder.

Add the dates and pulse slowly to incorporate. Follow with the tahini, one spoonful at a time, then the molasses. Keep pulsing until everything is well combined.

Toast the sesame seeds in a dry skillet over a low heat for a couple of minutes, or until they just turn golden. Spread them out in a layer on a flat plate and set aside to cool.

Use your palms to shape the date mixture into medium-sized balls (about 1 ½ tablespoons makes a good size), then roll them through the cooled sesame seeds until coated on all sides.

Spiced Dried Fruit Salad (Khoshaf)

خوشاف

 vegan   gluten-free

Traditionally, this is prepared in the evening before the first fasting day of Ramadan to be eaten in the predawn meal, not only because it tastes better after refrigerating, but also because it provides much-needed natural sugars, energy, and nutrients. We were told as kids that khoshaf has all the nourishment we needed for the day—not to mention that the prunes would keep us "regular." But this fruit salad can be prepared any time of the year, not least because the fruits, being dried, are always available. Every ingredient contributes to your overall health, but you can omit anything you don't like and it will still taste good. It's a great pre-workout snack, since dried fruits have concentrated levels of sugars and fiber that really boost vitality.

Makes: 6 servings

115 g (4 oz) dried apricots, halved (about ½ cup)

115 g (4 oz) dried pitted prunes, halved (about ½ cup)

115 g (4 oz) dried figs, quartered (about ½ cup)

3 cardamom pods

3 cloves

2–3 tablespoons raisins, or dried cranberries

2 tablespoons almonds, peeled

1–2 tablespoons pine nuts

1–2 teaspoons rose water, to taste

1 tablespoon date molasses (optional)

Time: 20 minutes

Wash the apricots, prunes, and figs in a sieve under cold running water and drain. Crush the cardamom pods with the back of a wooden spoon to open them up a little.

In a medium pan, place the apricots, prunes, and figs with the cardamom and cloves and cover with about 2 cups hot water. Bring to the boil, let simmer for about 5 minutes, then add the raisins (or cranberries) and simmer for another 5 minutes.

In a dry skillet over a medium heat, toast the almonds and pine nuts for a couple of minutes, shaking the pan so that none of them burn.

Add a drizzle of rose water and the toasted nuts to the hot fruits. Stir to combine, and remove the cloves and cardamom before serving. If extra sweetness is needed, drizzle over the date molasses. Serve warm or cold; it will keep in the fridge for up to 4 days.

Guava and Pomegranate Medley

 paleo   gluten-free

For us, fall brings the guava season, and families gorge on these luscious, fragrant fruits as well as filling their fridges with guava juice mixed with lime and sugar for a morning boost. It's perfect timing: these fruits are packed with vitamin C, so valuable for winter protection against colds and flu. The creamy sweet texture of guavas combined with the zesty crunch of pomegranate is ridiculously delicious, so simple and yet so refreshing. It will keep in your fridge for up to three days, and taste better by the day.

Makes: 6 generous servings

Seeds from 2–3 medium-sized
   pomegranates (about 2 cups)
6 medium guavas, peeled,
   deseeded, and cut into wedges
60 ml (¼ cup) orange juice
Juice of 2 limes
4 tablespoons raw honey
6–8 mint leaves, roughly torn or
   chopped

Time: 10 minutes + chilling time

Put the pomegranate seeds and two-thirds of the guava wedges into a medium serving bowl.

Put the remaining guava wedges, the orange and lime juice, the honey, and ½ cup cold water into a blender and blend to a smooth consistency. Pour this creamy juice over the fruit in the bowl.

Add the chopped mint and stir to combine. Chill for a couple of hours in the refrigerator before serving.

Roasted Figs and Nuts

تين مخبوز بالمكسرات

(🌾) gluten-free

This is not really a recipe, more the answer to a craving for something sweet and crunchy without any of the guilt! When late summer evenings at our beach house start to get a little chilly, we turn luscious fresh figs into this warm, simple dessert. It's a perfect way to transform the last of these glorious Mediterranean fruits into a special treat for ourselves and our guests—and it's so much cleaner and more wholesome than any refined, sugary confection.

We sometimes make this recipe more elaborate to create a more impressive dinner-party dish—caramelizing the nuts, for example, or crumbling some salty goat's cheese over the figs to melt as they roast—so feel free to experiment with your own twists.

Makes: 3–4 servings

6 figs (not too soft)
About 2 teaspoons ground
  cinnamon, to taste
Handful of shelled almonds,
  pecans, or pistachios (or a mix)
3 tablespoons raw honey

Time: 15 minutes

Preheat the oven to 180°C (350°F/Gas mark 4). Line an oven tray with baking parchment.

Wash the figs and cut just enough from the stem at the top to allow the figs to sit firmly upside-down on the tray. Use a sharp knife to cut a cross in the base of each, to about halfway down. Sprinkle in a little cinnamon, to taste. Place in the oven for about 10 minutes, until the figs are roasted and slightly softened.

While the figs roast, toast the nuts in a dry skillet over a medium heat for a couple of minutes. Remove from the heat and let them cool for a couple of minutes, then roughly chop them.

When the figs are ready, scatter the chopped nuts over them, then drizzle over the honey while the figs are still hot, and serve warm.

Orange Hibiscus Ice-pops

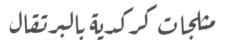

 paleo   ⊛ gluten-free

Refreshing, fun, and easy to prepare, these ice-pops are a summertime favorite. Kids love their sweet fruitiness, while adults are seduced by their tart berry and spice notes, so you can tailor the amount of honey you use to suit your audience.

Makes: 4 servings

2 tablespoons dried hibiscus flowers, or 4 hibiscus teabags
1 star anise
1 cm (½ in) piece of fresh ginger
2 tablespoons orange juice
2 teaspoons raw honey, or to taste

Time: 10 minutes + time to freeze

Put 2 cups water and hibiscus into a medium pan, and add the star anise and ginger. Bring to the boil, then lower the heat and let simmer uncovered for 5 minutes.

Remove from the heat, let it cool for just a couple of minutes, add the orange juice and honey, and stir. Once the honey is dissolved in the liquid, remove the hibiscus flowers or teabags, the ginger and star anise.

Let cool to room temperature, then pour into ice-pop molds, filling them only three-quarters of the way up: the liquid will expand as it freezes.

Put in the freezer for 2 hours minimum; once they're out, hand them around immediately!

Banana Nice Cream with Salted Caramel Pecans

الموز المثلج بالبيكان المكرمل

 vegan   Paleo

This 'no-recipe' dessert is the perfect savior for overripe bananas; there's no need ever to waste all the health benefits of this nutrient-packed fruit. In our house, any banana that's past its best gets squirreled away in the freezer so that we have a supply year-round for whipping up smoothies and 'nice creams'–just like ice cream, but dairy-free. This is one of our favorite nice cream flavors: a comforting mix of sweet banana and velvety vanilla concealing little crunchy chunks of caramelized pecan joy. But you can flavor it any way you like: add strawberries or cocoa at the blending stage; sprinkle it with toasted nuts, coconut shavings, or chocolate chips; or drizzle over some chocolate sauce or raw molasses.

Makes: 6 servings

5 overripe bananas
50 g (1.6 oz) pecans (about 1/3 cup) or walnuts
2 tablespoons raw molasses
Pinch of salt
2 tablespoons almond or oat milk
1 teaspoon vanilla extract

Time: 15 minutes + freezing and refrigerating time

Slice the bananas and lay them out, not touching each other, on an oven tray, then put the tray in the freezer for at least 2 hours. Freezing them this way prevents them from clumping together, which puts less strain on your food processor when you blend them. (If you're freezing banana for future use, then once the chunks are frozen, just tip them into a freezer bag and they'll stay separate.)

Before you prepare the nice cream, line a tray with baking parchment. Set aside.

Put the pecans or walnuts in a medium skillet over a medium heat, and drizzle over the molasses. Stir until all the nuts have a glossy, caramelized coating. Sprinkle the salt on top and give a final stir. Remove from the heat and tip the nuts onto the tray. Leave to cool, then roughly chop them.

Put the bananas, almond milk, and vanilla into a food processor and blend to a creamy texture. Sprinkle over the caramelized nuts and fold them in with a spoon or spatula. Spoon into a medium cake pan or serving bowl and freeze for 30 minutes. Flip the nice cream out into a flat serving dish or just serve straightaway, out of the mold or bowl.

Drinks المشروبات

Orange Blossom and Mint Lemonade

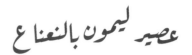

 gluten-free

Lemonade, or *lamonata*, is a popular summer drink in most Middle Eastern countries and, with its simplicity and freshness, it's popular with all the family. There are all sorts of twists on this classic drink, including blending it with milk or fresh mint. Here we keep it dairy- and sugar-free, yet sweet and refreshing, and instead of the traditional lemons, we've gone with limes, which are more commonly available in the Middle East. The raw honey combined with fragrant mint and orange blossom water in the cold lime juice is just heavenly!

Makes: 4 servings

Juice of 6–7 limes
2 tablespoons raw honey
250 ml (1 cup) warm water
1½ tablespoons orange blossom
   water (or to taste)
Handful of fresh mint leaves
1 teaspoon fresh ginger, grated
Handful of ice cubes

Time: 10 minutes

In a pitcher, mix the lime juice with 2 cups cold water.

In a separate pitcher or cup, dissolve the honey in the warm water, adding the orange blossom as you stir.

Pour the sweetened warm water into the first pitcher. Add the fresh mint leaves, ginger, and ice, stir, and serve straightaway.

Date Jallab

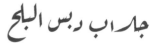

 vegan

Jallab is often made with pomegranate molasses, but in this version we use date molasses, packed with all the goodness and health benefits of dates, adding a little orange blossom water to create this perfumed thirst-quencher, rich in energy-boosting sugars. Both kids and grownups will enjoy this on a hot summer night.

Makes: 1 serving

2–3 tablespoons date molasses
180 ml (¾ cup) warm water
½ teaspoon orange blossom
  water
Ice cubes
1 teaspoon pine nuts

Time: 2 minutes

To a tall glass, add the date molasses, followed by ¾ cup warm water and orange blossom water. Stir until the molasses is completely dissolved, then add ice.

Toast pine nuts for a couple of minutes in a dry skillet on medium heat, then tip them over the jallab.

Cool Citrus Hibiscus

كركديه بالليمون

 paleo

Hibiscus tea has long been used as a traditional remedy in Middle Eastern countries for heart ailments and high blood pressure, and the most recent medical research seems to support this, while also suggesting that it may have a role to play in managing cholesterol levels and metabolic disorders. Hibiscus tea is also known as 'sour tea'; it's very tart, so it really needs the generous helping of honey we add here. In taste, it's most often compared to cranberry; we've added lime juice to accentuate its citrusy tones, plus warming cinnamon (which, like hibiscus, is packed with antioxidants), and stimulating ginseng. The result is an absolute cocktail of goodness with the most beautiful, ruby-red color. It will keep for up to two days in your fridge.

Makes: 1 liter (around 1 quart)

60 g (2 oz) dried hibiscus flowers (about 1 ½ cups)
2 ginseng stars or ½ teaspoon ground ginseng
2 cinnamon sticks, plus a couple to garnish
3 limes, 2 juiced and 1 sliced
4 tablespoons raw honey
Ice cubes

Time: 15 minutes + 1 hour to cool

In a medium pan over a high heat, bring 5 cups of water and the hibiscus to a boil. Add the ginseng and 2 cinnamon sticks, and lower the heat. Let it simmer uncovered for 10 minutes.

Remove from the heat, and strain into a bowl. While still warm, add the lime juice and honey, stirring until the honey dissolves.

Transfer to a pitcher or bottle, add the lime slices and fresh cinnamon sticks, and let it cool in the fridge for an hour before serving over ice.

Green Juice

عصير التفاح والخضرة

 vegan   paleo

This is a wonderfully healthy combination of greens, punchy and fragrant, and naturally sweetened by the fiber-full apple. Made fresh in the morning, it's a great wake-up drink that fuels you with energy and prepares you with a clean start to the day.

Ideally, use a juicer for this one, although with a couple of adjustments to the method, a power blender will do. You might also grate the ginger instead of adding it whole, to extract all its benefits.

Makes: 1 serving

1 apple, roughly chopped
1 stalk celery, chopped
1 lime, peeled
Generous handful of spinach
2 cm (1 in) piece of fresh ginger, peeled
1 cucumber, roughly chopped
Handful of mint leaves
4 medium ice cubes

Time: 10 minutes

Put all the ingredients except the ice cubes through a juicer, add the ice cubes, and serve straightaway.

If using a blender, add 125 ml (½ cup) cold water to the ingredients to help them mix. Blend until smooth and then strain through a sieve to remove any fibrous residue.

Creamy Spiced Mango Coconut Smoothie

عصير مانجة بجوز الهند

 vegan

Mangoes are such an important crop in our region. In summer, you'll see them piled high on market stalls in all their glorious variety, and every beach seems to have its own mango vendor, selling cups of luscious fruit or sweet juice. The extraordinary thing about mango juice is that it manages to be both refreshing and filling at the same time. This recipe, spicy and smooth with toasty coconut for texture, really is a meal in a cup. You can refrigerate it if you like (it will keep in the fridge for a couple of days), toasting the coconut flake garnish just before serving.

Makes: 1 large serving

1 medium mango, chopped
125 ml (½ cup) coconut milk
1 teaspoon grated fresh ginger
1 teaspoon grated fresh turmeric,
    or ½ teaspoon ground turmeric
½ teaspoon ground cardamom
½ teaspoon cinnamon
A grind of black pepper
4 small ice cubes, or 60 ml (¼
    cup) cold water
Coconut flakes, to garnish

Time: 5 minutes

Put all of the ingredients except the coconut flakes into a power blender and blend until smooth. If the consistency is too thick, add a couple more tablespoons of cold water.

In a dry skillet over a low heat, toast the coconut flakes for 2 minutes. Serve the smoothie in a large cup or glass, sprinkled with the warm toasted coconut.

Filling Sweet Date and Walnut Smoothie

عصير بلح بلبن اللوز

⊘ vegan   🛈 protein-packed   ⊗ paleo

Dates in every shape and form are a Middle Eastern delicacy, to be found growing on palm trees all over the region. There are so many varieties, differing in size, sweetness, and texture. Even Medjoul dates look and taste different in each country. This smoothie celebrates the date—its deliciousness, its high nutritional values, and its energy-boosting superpowers. This super-filling, wake-me-up smoothie could be used as a meal replacement, full of fiber, calcium, and protein. For best results, drink it straightaway. If you decide to keep it in the fridge before consuming, be sure to stir it or shake it before drinking!

Makes: 1 large serving

Small handful of walnuts
1 teaspoon flax seeds
250 ml (1 cup) cold almond milk
½ teaspoon cinnamon
6 Medjoul dates, pitted
½ banana
Handful of arugula

Time: 5 minutes

Put the walnuts and flax seeds into a power blender and pulse until finely ground (alternatively, blitz them in a food processor, then transfer to a blender). Add the cold almond milk and cinnamon and pulse to combine.

Add the dates, banana, and arugula, and blend for a full minute, until smooth. You may need to pause it occasionally to dislodge bits caught up at the bottom. Serve fresh.

Iced Turkish Coffee

قهوة مثلجة

⊘ vegan   ⧫ protein-packed

If you're a coffee-lover, then nothing else will do for that morning, noon, or afternoon pick-me-up, but when the temperatures rise, you want refreshment too. This heavenly cold coffee shot, creamed with almond milk and sweetened with diced dates, might just become your favorite summer energy drink. Try taking a flask to the beach!

You can always use a regular espresso shot for this recipe, but we urge you to try it with Arabic or Turkish coffee. When these spicy blends meet the dried dates, something really special happens.

Makes: 1 serving

2 dried or Medjoul dates
1 heaped teaspoon Turkish coffee
1–2 tablespoons cold almond
   milk (or more for a longer drink)
Ice cubes

Time: 10 minutes

Dice the dates and put them in the freezer to chill down fast.

To prepare the coffee, use your smallest milk pan to bring 125 ml (½ cup) water to a boil. Lower the heat to a simmer and add the Turkish coffee. Stir well to rehydrate the coffee and release its flavors. Let it simmer for a couple of minutes, or until you start to see an overlay of thickened coffee. Take it off the heat straightaway now, otherwise it might overflow.

Tip it in your serving cup, add as much cold almond milk as you like, and then some ice cubes. Add the frozen diced dates, stir, and enjoy.

Golden Milk

لبن اللوز الساخن بالبهارات

 vegan   paleo

Also known as turmeric tea, this is an ancient anti-inflammatory remedy, best drunk warm to maximize all the health benefits of turmeric (fighting some types of cancer is increasingly accepted as just one of them). The calcium-rich almond milk will give you all the comfort and goodness of a warm milky drink, without the dairy. Our kids love its creamy, spicy sweetness; it helps them relax before bed and gives their immune system a boost against coughs and colds while they sleep. To give the drink a little more pep, add a pinch of chili.

Makes: 1 serving

250 ml (1 cup) almond milk or coconut milk, or a mixture of both
1 teaspoon coconut oil
1 cm (½ in) piece of fresh ginger, grated, or ¼ teaspoon ground ginger
½ teaspoon cinnamon
½ teaspoon turmeric
A grind of black pepper
Raw honey, to taste
Pinch of chili (optional)

Time: 5 minutes

In a small pan, heat the almond milk, coconut oil, and ginger. Bring to the boil, then lower the heat and add the cinnamon, turmeric, and black pepper. Stir for half a minute, then remove from the heat. Strain out the ginger and add a teaspoon or two of raw honey to sweeten. You can also sprinkle in a pinch of chili if you like.

Index

Almond
  -crusted Sea Bass 172
  Gluten-free Granola Squares with
    Apricots and Prunes 50
Cinnamon and Sea-salt Butter 53
  Moroccan Chicken Fillets with Green
    Olive and Harissa Salsa 141
Almond Milk,
  Cauliflower, Garlic, and Almond Soup
    65
  Creamy Chestnut Soup 73
  Sweet Date and Walnut Smoothie 222
  Golden Milk 226
  Iced Turkish Coffee 225
  Spiced Date and Nut Cake 197
Apple
  Green Juice 218
Apricot
  Gluten-free Granola Squares with
    Prunes 50
  Moroccan Lamb Shoulder 152
  Spiced Dried Fruit Salad (Khoshaf) 201
Artichokes, Lime and Herb 116
Arugula
  Roasted Eggplants with Tahini and
    Pomegranate Molasses Dressing 30
  Bottarga Salad 47
Creamy Broccoli Soup 69
Beet and Mint Salad 87
Roasted Eggplant and Cauliflower Salad
  95
Avocado
  Chocolate Mousse with Fresh
    Pomegranate 189

Banana
  Spiced Date and Nut Cake 197
  Nice Cream with Salted Caramel
    Pecans 209
Beans,
  Green with Carrots and Tomatoes 124
  Green with Caramelized Onions 112

Spiced with Tahini 23
White (Butter) Bean Salad 92
White (Butter) Bean and Sundried
  Tomato Dip 43
see also Fava (Broad) Beans
Beef
  Bone Broth 59
Sea Salt Roast 155
  Casserole with Baby Carrots and
    Pickled Onions 157
  Maqluba Freekeh 158
  Eggplant Ground-meat Boats 164
  Chargrill-flavor Kofta 167
Beet
  and Mint Salad 87
  Lentil and Red Onion Salad 88
Belila, Chickpea 91
Bell Pepper
  Hummus Three Ways 19
  Oven-baked Calamari
  Tagine 181
Bessara 24
Black-eyed Pea and Spinach Stew 107
Bone Broth 59
Bottarga Salad 47
Broccoli
  Creamy Arugula Soup 69
  Street-style Crispy Baked Cauliflower
    and 115
Brussels Sprout
  Roasted Winter Vegetables with Sumac
    Vinaigrette 111

Cabbage, Walnut Rolls 131
Cake, Spiced Date and Nut 197
Calamari
  Oven-baked Tagine with Bell Peppers
    181
  Grilled, with Pomegranate Molasses
    and Chili 182
  Freekeh Paella 185
Capers, Smoked Herring with Tahini and 44

Carrot
  and Ginger Soup 67
  Roasted Winter Vegetables with Sumac
    Vinaigrette 111
  Sweet Potato and Herb Fritters 119
  Green Beans with Tomatoes and 124
  Beef Casserole with Pickled Onion 157
Casserole
  Beef with Baby Carrots and Pickled
    Onion 157
Cauliflower
  Garlic and Almond Soup 65
  Roasted Eggplant Salad 95
  Roasted Winter Vegetables with Sumac
    Vinaigrette 111
  Street-style Crispy Baked Broccoli and
    115
  Rice 128
  Maqluba Freekeh 158
Chard
  Khobeiza 127
Chargrill-flavor Kofta 167
Chestnut, Creamy Soup 73
Chicken
  Baked with Sweet Potato 137
  Messakhan 138
  Fillets with Green Olive and Harissa
    Salsa 141
  with Walnut Sauce (Sharkasiya) 142
  Molokhiya Bourani-style 145
  Livers with Pomegranate Molasses
    147
Chickpeas
  Hummus Three Ways 19
  Spicy Crispy 49
  Moroccan Soup 62
  Belila 91
  Freekeh and Lentil Koshari 99
  Moroccan Lamb Shoulder 152
  Maqluba 158
  Grilled Shrimp with a Cucumber Salad
    176

Chili
    Okra "Weika" 123
    Grilled Calamari with Pomegranate
    Molasses and 182
Chocolate
    Avo-mousse with Fresh Pomegranate
    189
    Tahini Squares 194
Cinnamon
    and Sea-salt Almond Butter 53
    and Pomegranate Molasses Roasted
    Quail 151
Clams
    Freekeh Paella 185
Coconut milk
    Spiced Brown Rice Pudding 193
Creamy Spiced Mango Smoothie 221
Coffee
    Iced Turkish 225
Coriander
    Baked Whole Fish with Tahini and 171

Dates
    Fried Eggs with 39
    Tahini Cups 190
    Spiced Nut Cake 197
    Walnut and Seed Energy Balls 198
    Jallab 214
    Filling Sweet Walnut Smoothie 222
    Iced Turkish Coffee 225

'Eggah 35
Eggplant
    Roasted with Tahini and Pomegranate
    Molasses Dressing 30
    Smoked Dip 33
    Warm Lentil and Pomegranate Salad
    81
    Roasted Cauliflower Salad 95
    Warm Freekeh Salad 96
    Vegan Moussaka 120
    Maqluba Freekeh 158
    Ground-meat Boats 164
Eggs
    Green 'Eggah 35
    Mediterranean Omelet with Goat's Milk
    Feta 36
    Fried with Dates 39
    Vegetable-filled Shakshouka 40

Falafel
    Egyptian with Green Onion and Tomato
    27
    Baked Yellow Lentil 29
Fattoush Salad 83

Fava (Broad) Beans
    Spiced with Tahini 23
    Bessara 24
    Egyptian Falafel with Green Onion and
    Tomato 27
Fennel
    Roasted Winter Vegetables with Sumac
    Vinaigrette 111
Feta
    Mediterranean Omelet 36
    Greek Fig Salad 84
Figs
    Greek Salad 84
    Spiced Dried Fruit Salad (Khoshaf) 201
    Roasted Nuts 205
Fish,
    Almond-crusted Sea Bass 172
    Baked Whole, with Tahini and
    Coriander 171
    Cakes, with Sweet Potato and Herbs
    175
Freekeh
    Warm Eggplant Salad 96
    Lentil and Chickpea Koshari 99
    Maqluba 158
    Paella 185

Garlic
    Cauliflower and Almond Soup 65
    Freekeh, Lentil, and Chickpea Koshari
    99
    Molokhiya Bourani-style 145
Ginger
    and Carrot Soup 67
    Shrimp with Warm Lentils 179
Granola, Gluten-free Squares with
    Apricots and Prunes 50
Green Beans
    with Caramelized Onions 112
    with Carrots and Tomatoes 124
Greek Fig Salad 84
Guava and Pomegranate Medley 202

Harissa, Moroccan Chicken Fillets with
    Green Olive and Salsa 141
Herring, Smoked with Tahini and Capers
    44
Hibiscus
    Orange Ice-pops 206
    Cool Citrus 217
Hummus Three Ways 19

Jallab, Date 214
Juice, Green 218

Khobeiza 127
Khoshaf (Spiced Dried Fruit Salad) 201
Kofta, Chargrill-flavor 167
Koshari, Freekeh, Lentil and Chickpea 99

Lamb
    Vine Leaf Pie 104
    Moroccan Shoulder 152
Lentils
    with Parsley 17
    Spiced Beans with Tahini 23
    Baked Yellow Falafel 29
    Vegetable Soup 61
    Warm Eggplant and Pomegranate
    Salad 81
    Beet and Red Onion Salad 88
    Freekeh and Chickpea Koshari 99
    Ginger Shrimp with 179
Lettuce, Herby Turkey Burgers 148
Lime
    Pickled, with Quinoa Tabbouleh 78
    and Herb Artichokes 116
    Cauliflower Rice 128

Mallow
    Molokhiya Bourani-style 145
Mango
    Creamy Spiced Coconut Smoothie 221
Maqluba Freekeh 158
Mediterranean Omelet with Goat's Milk
    Feta 36
Mint
    and Beet Salad 87
Orange Blossom Lemonade 213
Molokhiya Bourani-style 145
Moussaka, Vegan 120
Mussels
    Freekeh Paella 185

Oats
    Date and Tahini Cups 190
Okra, Chili "Weika" 123
Olives
    Moroccan Chicken Fillets with Harissa
    Salsa 141
Onion
    Traditional Salad with Tomato 77
    Lentil, Beet, and Red Onion Salad 88
    Freekeh, Lentil and Chickpea Koshari 99
    Quinoa-stuffed Caramelized 103
    Green Beans with Caramelized 112
    Pickled, in Beef Casserole with Baby
    Carrots157
Onion, green
    Egyptian Falafel with Tomato and 27

Orange, Hibiscus Ice-pops 206
Orange Blossom, and Mint Lemonade
  213

Paella, Freekeh 185
Parsley, Easy Lentils with 17
Pecans, Banana Nice Cream with Salted
  Caramel 209
Pie, Vine Leaf 104
Pomegranate
  Roasted Eggplants with Tahini and
  Molasses Dressing 30
  Warm Lentil and Eggplant Salad 81
  Warm Freekeh and Eggplant Salad 96
  Chicken Livers with Molasses 147
  Cinnamon and Molasses Roasted
  Quails 151
  Grilled Calamari with Molasses and
  Chili 182
  Avo-chocolate Mousse 189
  and Guava Medley 202
Prunes
  Gluten-free Granola Squares with
  Apricots and 50
  Spiced Dried Fruit Salad (Khoshaf) 201
Pumpkin, Spiced Soup 70

Quail, Roasted with Cinnamon and
  Pomegranate Molasses 151
Quinoa
  Tabbouleh with Pickled Lime 78
  -stuffed Caramelized Onions 103
  Vine Leaf Pie 104
  Walnut Cabbage Rolls 131
  White Fish Cakes with Sweet Potato
  and Herbs 175

Raisins
  Spiced Dried Fruit Salad (Khoshaf) 201
Rice
  Cauliflower 128

Spiced Brown Rice Pudding 193

Sea Bass
  Baked Whole with Tahini and Coriander
  171
  Almond-crusted 172
  White Fish Cakes with Sweet Potato
  and Herbs 175
Sea Salt
  Cinnamon Almond Butter 53
  Roast Beef 155
Sesame Seeds
  Walnut and Seed Energy Balls 198
Sharkasiya 142
Shrimp
  Grilled with a Chickpea and Cucumber
  Salad 176
  Ginger with Warm Lentils 179
  Freekeh Paella 185
Spinach
  Black-eyed Pea Stew 107
  Chips 133
  Herby Turkey Burgers in Lettuce Wraps
  148
  Green Juice 218
Strawberry, Homemade Jam 54
Sumac
  Roasted Winter Vegetables with
  Vinaigrette 111
  Chicken Messakhan 138
Slow-cooked Veal Shanks 163
Sweet Potato
  Hummus Three Ways 19
  Carrot and Herb Fritters 119
  Baked Chicken with 137
  White Fish Cakes with Herbs 175

Tabbouleh, Quinoa with Pickled Lime 78
Tahini
  Hummus Three Ways 19
  Spiced Beans with 23

Roasted Eggplants with Pomegranate
  Molasses Dressing 30
Smoked Herring with Capers 44
Baked Whole Fish with Coriander 171
Date Cups 190
Chocolate Squares 194
Tomato
  Egyptian Falafel with Green Onion and 27
  White Bean Dip 43
  and Onion Salad 77
  Quinoa-stuffed Caramelized Onions
  103
  Freekeh, Lentil and Chickpea Koshari
  99
  Black-eyed Pea and Spinach Stew 107
  Vegan Moussaka 120
  Green Beans with Carrots and 124
  Moroccan Chicken Fillets with Green
  Olive and Harissa Salsa 141
  Slow-cooked Veal Shanks 163
  Oven-baked Calamari and Bell Pepper
  Tagine 181
Turkey, Herby Burgers in Lettuce Wraps 148

Veal, Slow-cooked Shanks 163
Vegetables, Roasted with Sumac
  Vinaigrette 111
Vegetable-filled Egg Shakshouka 40
Vine Leaf Pie 104

Walnuts
  Greek Fig Salad 84
  Green Beans with Caramelized Onions
  112
  Cabbage Rolls 131
  Chicken Breast with Walnut Sauce
  (Sharkasiya) 142
  Date and Tahini Cups 190
  Spiced Date and Nut Cake 197
  and Seed Energy Balls 198
  Filling Sweet Date Smoothie 222